The Word and Wax

A Medical Folk Ritual Among Ukrainians In Alberta

Second edition

Canadian Series in Ukrainian Ethnology

Volume II

Volume editor
Andriy Nahachewsky

Series founding editor
Bohdan Medwidsky

The Word and Wax

A Medical Folk Ritual Among Ukrainians In Alberta

Second edition

Rena Jeanne Hanchuk

KIYC
CIUS

Canadian Institute of Ukrainian Studies Press
and Kule Folklore Centre
Edmonton 2023 Toronto

Canadian Institute of Ukrainian Studies Press

University of Alberta
Edmonton, Alberta
T6G 2H8 CANADA

University of Toronto
Toronto, Ontario
M5S 2C3 CANADA

Huculak Chair of Ukrainian Culture and Ethnography

University of Alberta, Edmonton, Alberta, CANADA T6G 2E6

ISBN 978-1-894865-67-8 (pbk.)

Library and Archives Canada Cataloguing in Publication

Title: The word and wax: a medical folk ritual among Ukrainians in Alberta / Rena Jeanne Hanchuk.
Names: Hanchuk, Rena Jeanne, 1960- author. | University of Alberta. Canadian Institute of Ukrainian Studies, publisher.
Description: Second edition. | Includes bibliographical references and index.
Identifiers: Canadiana 2023049983X | ISBN 9781894865678 (softcover)
Subjects: LCSH: Beeswax—Therapeutic use. | LCSH: Traditional medicine—Alberta. | LCSH: Ukrainians—Medicine. | LCSH: Ukrainians—Folklore.
Classification: LCC GR113.7.U57 H35 2023 | DDC 398/.353—dc23

The cover illustration is taken from "Vorozhka" (The Soothsayer), a painting by Jeanette Shewchuk of Warren, Manitoba. It is reproduced courtesy of the Canadian Museum of Civilization, neg. no. K86-594.

Printed in Canada

This work is dedicated to the memory of my maternal grandmother, Maria Kapitska-Cholak, who instilled in me a love for things Ukrainian; and to Mrs. V. B., whose help my grandmother encouraged me to seek and who twelve years later became the central figure of this work.

Foreword

An earlier version of this monograph was defended in 1990 as an M.A. thesis in the Ukrainian Folklore Program in the Department of Slavic and East European Studies at the University of Alberta. We are pleased to be able to support Ukrainian and Canadian ethnology by making this study available to the public.

Andriy Nahachewsky
Volume Editor

Contents

The Healer:
Preface to the Second Edition

***The healer**: well-versed in herbs, who knows through experience the roots, the trees, the stones. She is experienced, tests her remedies, examines, keeps her secrets, her traditions.*
***The good healer**: cures people, helps them, puts them on their feet, eases their bodies, brings them to convalescence, covers their wounds with ashes, cures, remedies, makes incisions, draws the blood, sews, purges people, gives them remedies.*

Attributes of Aztec physicians and healers as described in the Florentine Codex.

50 years ago, when I was 12 years old, my maternal grandmother, Maria Kapitski-Cholak, told my mama to take me to a wax pourer. A babka could take away the fear with which I was evidently living and which was manifesting itself in sleepless nights and a nervous condition that had me biting my nails, twirling my hair on my fingers, and chewing my tongue.

"*Bery Rinku do babtsi aby toi strakh zlyla. Vona khodyt do nashoi tserkvy. Babka Vasylyna. To vse sho treba.*" I remember baba's words as if they were spoken just yesterday. "*Take her to a healer to have her pour out the fear. She attends our church. Her name is healer Vasylyna. It's all she (Rena) needs.*"

I visited babka Vasylyna several times to exorcise the fear that I had growing in me. Somehow babka Vasylyna, or Violet, was able to calm me down with her wax and her prayers. I would carry a fascination for the Wax Ceremony with me years later, all the way to the University of Alberta, where in 1978 I began taking courses in Ukrainian languages and folklore. It was there that I revisited the Wax Ceremony as a topic when I began discussing it with my professors. I took many courses in the Department of Slavic and East European Studies, as it was called at that time. Eventually, I would earn a bachelor's degree in Ukrainian studies and folklore and go on to defend a master's thesis about the Wax Ceremony in 1990, entitled "Folk Psychology and Ukrainians in Alberta." Of all the types of remedies the Ukrainians had brought with them, what was so special about the Wax Ceremony? Why had it survived while other types of healing had waned or ceased to exist? These questions still haunt me to this day.

In 1999, I was contacted by the Huculak Chair of Ukrainian Culture and Ethnography and the Canadian Institute of Ukrainian Studies at the University of Alberta. They encouraged me to tweak my thesis, rename and publish it! It would become the current book: *The Word and Wax: A Medical Folk Ritual Among Ukrainians in Alberta.* I would become a published author, releasing a book about my beloved Wax Ceremony at the age of 39. How exciting! The book would go on to be sold for decades and slowly gain popularity with the public.

Now, in 2022, my precious book is being reprinted 23 years later because there still is an interest in this Ukrainian phenomenon. The book still has a following and there is a new generation of folks who are interested in the book, in the ceremony, in the wax. I am still contacted by individuals who want to buy the book or who have questions for me about the Wax Ceremony. They find me in a variety of ways and I get one to two inquiries a month! Imagine! 50 years later and I am still involved with the Wax Ceremony. I have met with numerous people who want to learn how to pour wax, interpret the figures in the wax or to go to a healer who is still practicing. Who would have guessed that in this modern time of ours there still would be such interest in an ancient medicine?

My favorite gal who reaches out to me is a witch with a witchery store in Edmonton where she has sold dozens of copies of the book! There have been reviews done on the book, and papers that quote the book extensively as a reference. One such example is, "Waxing Like the Moon: Women Folk Healers in Rural Western Ukraine," by Sarah D. Phillips from the University of Indiana. There even was an MA project written recently at the University of Alberta about the Wax Ceremony and how it has remained or changed since my original book was written!

There seems to be a new generation of people interested in traditional healing and folkways, and the Wax Ceremony and its healers speak to them. I met with a rather young woman who pours wax for people and practices the Wax Ceremony simply by reading the incantations that are found in my book, the *Word and Wax*.

It is with a great deal of gratitude that I find myself writing this preface before a second edition of something that started more than 50 years ago out of my own insomnia and fears. Thank you to CIUS for moving the *Word and Wax* along for those who will follow the Wax Ceremony as babas of a new generation! Draw the water, melt the wax, utter your incantations, interpret the moulded figurines, and heal on!

As many of the babas incant, "*Shchezai i propadai ...lehku nich mai!" May your fears disappear and go amiss...have a good sleep!*

Blessings,
Rena Jeanne Hanchuk, M.A., B.A. Hon., B.Ed

Acknowledgements

I express my deepest gratitude to the dozens of individuals and organizations that provided me with moral and financial support and thereby helped me to fulfill my dream.

I acknowledge my thesis supervisor, Dr. Bohdan Medwidsky, for his patience and genuine interest in my work.

I thank the Division of Slavic and East European Studies, University of Alberta, for its financial and moral support; the Historic Sites Services, Alberta Culture and Multiculturalism, for its financial support; St. John's Institute, Edmonton, for awarding me the S. F. Woloshyn scholarship; and the Sudbury, Ontario branch of the Ukrainian Profes- sional and Businessmen's Club for awarding me the J. Syroid Scholar- ship.

The Ukrainian Museum of Canada in Saskatoon kindly supplied me with research materials. A special note of appreciation is due to librarian Mrs. Marion Lake, who diligently acquired interlibrary loan materials for me during my stay at the University of Regina.

For his technical advice, I acknowledge the assistance of Radomir Bilash. I thank my proofreaders, Dr. Gust Olson and Marie Lesoway, who scrutinized every word of my thesis. In the final weeks of editing and correcting before its defense, they held my hand and my spirit-together we burned the midnight wax.

I thank Mrs. N. D. and her family for their co-operation and opening their hearts and their doors to me. I also thank my thirty-one informants for their belief and their willingness to openly share their convictions. Gratitude is also due to the secondary informants who served as patients during several interviews.

I warmly thank the healers who shared their secrets, power, and prayers with me.

Last, but far from least, I thank my family for their guidance, and my parents, who planted the seed that became this study.

List of Illustrations and Tables

Introduction

A fascinating medical folk ritual called *vylyvaty visk* or *strakh vylyvaty* is known among Ukrainians in Alberta. A loose English translation of the name would be "the pouring forth of wax" or "the pouring forth of fear." This ritual will be called the "wax ceremony" in this study.

During the wax ceremony, a patient who comes to a healer for help is seated in a chair. A bowl is filled with cold water, and a lump of wax is melted. The healer engages in conversation and asks the patient for his or her symptoms. An incantation is uttered, and the wax is poured into the water over the head of the patient. The solidified wax is taken from the water and turned over, and its shapes are interpreted. This process is typically repeated three times. The ceremony is considered effective in curing fear sickness and numerous other maladies.

The wax ceremony is a magico-religious and oral-incantational genre of folk medicine. Depending on the healer, the ceremony is invested with Christian as well as pre-Christian imagery. The cure often involves divining the source of the illness. The ceremony can also be perceived as a genre of oral literature, because it is always performed with an accompanying ritual prayer or incantation. The oral formula contains religious and parareligious symbols. In order to bring about a cure, the healer fuses magic, religion, formula, and faith.

The wax ceremony is part of a rich folkloric tradition brought to Alberta by an agrarian people who emigrated primarily from the western regions of Ukraine starting near the turn of this century.[1] This type of folk medicine was widely practiced in Ukraine and was easily transplanted to the new homeland. Other Old Country folk remedies required herbs, plasters, or other materials that were not easily obtainable in Alberta. The wax ceremony, however, could be practised readily by a healer armed with an appropriate incantation, water, and beeswax. It has clearly found a home in Alberta, where it reflects its Ukrainian origins as well as its contemporary Canadian context.

---

1. The first wave of emigration from Ukraine to Alberta began in 1891. For descriptions of Ukrainian Canadian history, see Martynowych 1991 and Tesla et al. 1971, 1151–93.

The wax ceremony was important at the time of immigration and in the years that immediately followed. It nullified fear, nervousness, sleeplessness, and restlessness, social and psychological disorders that occurred among people who had emigrated to a strange and foreign land. The ceremony was a culturally meaningful method of reducing stress and anxiety. The healers externalized these afflictions with their treatments and restored a sense of normality in their patients. They provided an effective mechanism for coping and served an important social role within the community.

Health is not entirely an objective and physical state. It also involves many culturally based factors. The Ukrainian immigrants to Canada shared specific, elaborate cultural ideas about health, illness, and the causes of disease. It is logical that they would choose health practitioners who shared their primary medical assumptions. The immigrants' financial status and inability to communicate in English would also have accentuated the need for Ukrainian lay healers in the early years of settlement. Consequently the wax ceremony not only flourished in Alberta, but grew to become an integral and dynamic component of the entire transposed folklore complex. It remains a widespread and popular practice today.

Only a few works have been written on the wax ceremony in western Canada. They include unpublished research papers by Rena Hanchuk (1984a, 1984b) and Lori-Lee Chomik (1982). Andrea K. Klymasz mentions it in her brief article (1989) and her M.A. thesis (1991). Robert B. Klymasz's *Sviéto* (1992) contains numerous brief descriptions and discussions of wax pouring. The ceremony is also described in several Ukrainian Canadian literary works (Lysenko 1954; Gulutsan 1978; Kostash 1980; Galay 1981).

The literature on folk medicine in Ukraine contains much relevant information, including occasional descriptions of the wax ceremony or its elements. Publications before 1917 (Dmitriukov 1831; Arandarenko [1849] 1979; Chubinskii [1872] 1979; Efimenko 1874; Kertselli 1874; Dragomanov 1876; Bogdanovich 1877; Podolinskii 1879; Brailovskii 1891; Kovalenko and Manzhura 1891; Kolberg [1889] 1963; "Novinki" 1893; Miloradovich 1900; V. K. 1902; Domanyts'kyi 1905; Shukhevych 1908) and from outside the Soviet bloc (Nedzel's'kyi 1955; "Chary" 1961) are of a markedly different character from the few publications from Soviet Ukraine (Porits'kyi and Prykhod'ko 1965; Dumka 1968; Boltarovych 1980, 1983, 1987).

Researchers of the wax ceremony can also find relevant information in publications on related topics: folk religion (Jones 1972), the evil eye (Maloney 1976; Dundes 1981), witchcraft (Ehrenreich 1973), fortune telling (Moore 1957), superstitions, and children's lore. Some sources deal with folk healing or folk religion in Slavic culture in general (Moszyński [1934] 1967, 175–232; Tokarev 1957, 124–34; Petroff 1957; Pondoev 1959; Drazheva 1973; Bromlei 1976) or the folk medicine of a related Slavic culture (Afanas'ev [1865–9] 1970, 364–431; Sokolov [1938] 1950, 241–57; Min'ko 1969). A number of works dealing with folk healing in other Slavic communities in North America are also relevant to this study (for example, Stein 1976).

The bulk of information for this study was gathered from practitioners in the community. Seven healers were interviewed as primary informants; six of them were still practicing at that time. Twenty-one patients of such healers provided information as secondary informants. Relatives and acquaintances of the patients also helped in the research. The participants ranged in age from twenty-four to ninety-three. Several have since passed away. All but two were residents of Edmonton or east central Alberta. Twenty-four were women; sixteen were men. All of the informants were of Ukrainian ancestry. Nine were born in Ukraine; two of them had emigrated only recently. The informants' economic and social status varied.

Several unrecorded interviews were conducted by telephone or in person. Some thirty more formal interviews were recorded on audio or video tapes. Interviews were based on questionnaires to allow for more complete and consistent information collection. Two healers allowed me to make video recordings as they performed the wax ceremony.[2] The researcher accompanied patients to three different rural healers and observed their interaction.

---

2. Interviews with informants have been numbered to correspond with the interview and tape numbers in the Ukrainian Folklore Archives in the Department of Modern Languages and Cultural Studies at the University of Alberta, where the original tapes are housed (accession no. 1986.006). All relevant interview tapes have been transcribed and, if conducted in Ukrainian, translated. See the list of interviews.

Many of the informants were uncomfortable with having their interviews recorded. Three of the healers refused to be interviewed on tape; however, they allowed me to observe them performing the wax ceremony. One informant tried to disguise her voice while she was interviewed, and she refused to provide any personal information. Many informants requested that their names not be disclosed. The informants are therefore referred to by initials. In many instances, they expressed concern that personal information could be misinterpreted or ridiculed by educated people and that, in any case, such information had no place in scholarly research.

The first chapter of this study deals with folk medicine and its relationship with official Western medicine and Christianity as an "official religion." Various important elements of the wax ceremony are introduced in the second chapter. The ceremony itself is described in detail in chapter three, while chapter four deals specifically with the incantations. The final chapter raises issues of the survival of the ritual and its viability today. A glossary of relevant Ukrainian terms is included.

I agree with my informants that a large chasm exists between their type of knowledge and the "scholarly world" as they perceive it. These are, perhaps, truly different worlds. My intent is to help bridge that gap and to make this knowledge comprehensible to everyone.

Folk Medicine

Health and illness are culturally relative concepts. People's actions during illness are influenced by standards in the society in which they live (Blum and Blum 1965, 142). The patient plays a role that is learned as part of his or her culture.

The term "medicine" may have a broader scope in some cultures than in others (Toelken 1979, 226). In some cultures, for example, medicine may be used for protection, to will luck, to calm evil spirits, or to procure love. Contemporary Western definitions of medicine exclude such activities. One thing is clear: in order to understand and appreciate other medical cultures, we must look beyond our own definitions of medicine. "[In Western medicine] our experience stops at the frontiers of the natural. The most important part of ... [a person's experience in other cultures may be] on the other side of this frontier in his contact with the dead, the spirits, and mystic ancestors. What for us is a mere hallucination is for him a privileged experience" (Ackernecht 1942, 506).

"Herbal" and "Magico-Religious" Medicine

Western writings on folk medicine often divide the field into two categories: "rational," "natural," or "herbal" medicine on the one hand, and "irrational," "occult," or "magico-religious" medicine on the other (Yoder 1972, 192). "Rational" or "herbal" medicine refers to medical practices using plants, herbs, and other natural substances available in the surrounding environment. Such practices originated in times immemorial. They developed through keen observation, trial and error, and deduction. People discovered that some substances, when used in certain ways, produced specific results. Some of these results were desirable; others were not. If applied appropriately, knowledge of them could be used to help heal oneself, one's family, and one's animals if they fell ill. People discovered that many plants had a great healing potential.

In the evolution of folk medicine, first herbs were gathered. Later they were actively cultivated for medicinal use. "Herbs that were thought to give them [women] special curative ability were gathered in woodland and field, in the fall or on certain days of the church year, and the women planted herb gardens that were used for medical much more than for culinary purposes" (Yoder 1972, 198). Aside from herbs, the so-called herbal medicinal practices involved animal matter and inorganic material (Yoder 1972, 192; Boltarovych 1980, 78–93).

"Magico-religious" medicine, on the other hand, involves the use of non-material means to cure illness. Man believed some 5,000 years ago that his health depended on his state of mind. "Men were healed of their diseases by non-physical methods directed towards their minds rather than their bodies. They sought to integrate the wholeness of personality" (Weatherhead 1952, 27–8).

Boltarovych writes about the development of folk medicine in relation to pre-Christian religion in Ukraine: "Curative magic as a branch of folk medicine appeared in those ancient times when man, unable to understand the laws of nature and being helpless before the surrounding elements, personified and animated them and populated the world with supernatural beings and spirits" (Boltarovych 1980, 10).

Over time the identity of the spirits and beings crystallized in the minds of the people. Whole religious systems were developed, involving sometimes a complex hierarchy of gods, spirits, minor deities, and other supernatural forces. Each of these forces may have been perceived to have their own personality, needs, desires, likes, and dislikes. The supernatural world, the natural world, and humanity were perceived as being tightly interconnected. People believed that events in one sphere influenced events in the others. Malady was thought to result from the displeasure of the gods. Illness and disease were punishment for the misalignment with that world (Hand 1980, 57–8). The converse was also true. People believed that certain words, actions, thoughts, times, places, and relationships in the natural world could influence the spiritual entities and their attitudes in positive ways. A man, for example, could make offerings to help ensure that he, his family, and his chattels would not fall out of favour with the gods.

The extent of the perception of the interrelationship between man and the spirit world is attested to by the ancient folk-medicine phenomenon known as the evil eye. Traditions relating to the evil eye have been found in most cultures over millennia. They are documented in the Bible, the Apocrypha, and the Koran. A man could harm humans and animals alike by casting an evil glance (Dundes 1980, 94). The glance was made evil by spirits who could be appeased by incantations or warded off by wearing special amulets. Such talismans and amulets have been worn since Paleolithic times (Weatherhead 1952, 27).

In practice, the division between herbal and magico-religious medicine is artificial. In fact, they are intricately interwoven. In the context of herbal medicine, a leaf might be understood to have curative power. In the realm of magico-religious medicine, the same leaf is seen to be curative when one applies it to a wound while intoning an accompanying prayer. Folk-medicine practitioners may be quite aware of the importance of the interplay between magic and herbal remedies. They perceive remedies as effective not solely because of the plants and herbs used, but also because of the power of the incantation, the actions, and other factors.

The Folk Healer

Some folk medicine is common knowledge within a society, and can be performed by almost anyone. However, home remedies do not always result in a cure. Specialized members of the community may then be called upon. The skills of such specialists may be attributed to their greater experience and knowledge, but often also to their talent or innate powers. A Wise Man or Wise Woman is endowed with an especial rapport with the spiritual world. He or she can communicate with that world and pacify the spirits, thereby restoring health and equilibrium to the society. Specialist healers have been recognized for 30,000 years (Camp 1978, 12).

Barbara Myerhoff writes about the importance that such individuals have in the restoration of health or normality within the clan. The folk healer

> as a connector is bridging the primordial past and the mythical past with historical time. He is at the same time mastering psychological transitions.... And in carrying out his cures, he accomplishes social equilibrium as well by establishing balance between the individual and his group, by

> reweaving the social texture that has been ruptured by illness and frequently by some violation of group norms that causes the sickened individual to be seen and treated as a deviant.... As a connecting figure, he is at once the restorer of balance and the symbol of the possibility of balance. In his cosmic undertakings, his personal destiny mirrors his profession, and the microcosm and macrocosm are reunited by his activities. (Myerhoff 1976, 100)

The healer's function is not limited to his or her relationship with the sick. These activities are important for the society as a whole. When all members of a given society or clan are healthy, harmony and rhythm are established in the community. Once a member falls ill, however, rhythm is disrupted. The person must be cared for, and sometimes his or her role in society must be temporarily assumed by other members so that the cycle of food production or caring for the young may remain intact. The folk healer can restore order by pacifying the necessary spirits, eliminating the state of disease (dis-ease) and restoring harmony (Tillich 1946, 354–5). Because they are the agents through which the patient's recovery is made possible, the healers are a mainstay of social order within a culture. They reintegrate their patients into health and normality and thus restore the equilibrium of their society.

In the wax ceremony, the healer is usually a woman. The nomenclature of these healers in Ukrainian is quite extensive: *baba* (old woman); *babka*, *babtsia*, and *babunia* (old woman, diminutive); *baba-povytukha* (old woman, midwife); *baila* (murmurer); *chaklunka*, *charivnytsia*, and *charnytsia* (conjurer); *chudesnytsia* (wonder-worker); *koldunytsia* (sorceress); *obavnytsia* (conjurer); *potvornytsia* (seer); *proklinnytsia* (witch); *prymivnytsia* (sorceress); *sheptukha* (murmurer); *starukha* and *starushka* (old woman); *vid'ma* (witch); *vidunka* (wise woman/witch); *vishchunytsia* (wise woman); *vorozhka*, *vorozhbytka*, and *vorozhylia* (fortune-teller/witch); *vydunytsia* (wise woman); *zhena-vorozhylia* (witch); *znakha* and *znakharka* (wise woman); and *zolotarykha* (golden conjurer).

These appellations have been translated loosely. For the most part, they are used interchangeably.[3] The most commonly used appellation for the Ukrainian healer in western Canada is "*baba.*"

While many of the patients who were interviewed for this study claimed that even the researcher should be able to learn how to pour wax effectively, the majority felt that healers were chosen by God because of their special qualities. They believe that the oldest or youngest child in a family has special healing abilities. All of Mrs. V. B.'s family members referred to this belief. Mrs. J. T. looked for crosses on the left hand of a potential healer. If there were three crosses, she believed that the individual had the ability to cure. Mrs. J. T. also said that in addition to possessing these special crosses, she was also endowed with powers because she was the thirteenth child in her family.

According to Hand, "The folk healer's art is acquired in two ways, but essentially the endowment falls into three main categories, namely a gift specially conferred, one innate in the healer, or one resulting from some unique condition, a new acquired status or even happenstance" (Hand 1980, 44).

Folk healers have usually kept their healing art a strict secret (cf, Podolinskii 1879, 18b). They have not advertised their services and are reluctant to share their incantations and rituals. This kind of reticence was encountered among the healers interviewed for this study. One healer said that he could not share his incantation with anyone lest he should lose his power to heal. He threatened the researcher with spells if she tried to harm him or his powers (Interview 14). Another healer said that if she told anyone her incantations, she would lose her powers. She said that when she was ready to retire she would pass on her incantations. Until such time the words to her incantation, together with the names of three healers whom she had chosen to continue her healing

3. Information about the etymology of many of these appellations is given by Ralston ([1872] 1970, 378–9). He says that *vedun* (wizard) and *ved'ma* (witch) come from *ved*, which is derived from Sanskrit *vid* (knowledge). In Ukrainian, the noun *visti* (news) is derived from the same root. Similarly, *znakhar/znakharka* can be traced to the root *znat'* (to know). Ralston says that the etymology of *koldun/koldunia* is not understood by scholars. He offers Sreznevskii's theory that a *koldun* was one who made sacrifices to the gods. He points out that in Croatian *kaldovati* is a verb that means to sacrifice; a priest is known as *kaldovanets*; and *charovnik/charovnitsa* is derived from *char* (spell).

after her death, were locked in a safety-deposit box. Mrs. V. B. "stole" her incantations from her mother-in-law, who refused to teach her. She learned the special incantations by listening as the ceremony was performed. A relative of one of the interviewed healers advised that once she had passed on her entire incantation, the healer, relieved of the burden to heal, would be free to die. Shortly after the final interviews for this study were completed, she passed away. Her relatives found it difficult not to associate the researcher with the cause of the healer's death.

Folk Medicine and Official Western Medicine

When contrasted with modern scientific medicine and pharmacology, folk medicine is often viewed as quackery or unorthodox in nature (Camp 1978, 82–4). It should not be forgotten, however, that scientific medicine is relatively new compared to the centuries of healing that have preceded it. In any event, its roots, too, lie in lay healing (Porits'kyi and Prykhod'ko 1965, 70).

The beginnings of Western medicine are often associated with the Greek healer Hippocrates (c. 470/460–377 B.C.). Hippocrates was a keen observer and worked systematically to understand the process of cause and effect in his medicinal practice. He de-emphasized the magico-religious aspect of healing. He and his school of medical practitioners were qualitatively different than the others; "scientific" medicine was starting to be contrasted with "folk" medicine. People associated with the former were accorded higher status (Weatherhead 1952, 30). A new hierarchy of medicine began forming. Hippocrates made such an impact and contribution to modern medicine that his oath to medicine and humankind is still taken by medical students today.

Of course, even as Hippocrates' practices developed into the official medicine of today, they did not replace the folk medicine that existed before and alongside them. Folk medicine has been intricately connected with the worldview of its practitioners about both the natural and the unseen. It has been impossible to uproot centuries of tradition and belief.

The methods employed by the folk healer may not be compatible with the official scientific explanation for disease causation or cure, but this may be of little significance to patients. If they believe, the method tends to work. Thus the streams of official and unofficial medicine have continued to develop with somewhat parallel histories. Sometimes they have coexisted in harmony and agreement; sometimes they have operated in opposition to each other as competitors for status, each claiming primary legitimacy. In most cases of conflict, of course, official medicine has driven the folk practice underground.

Not all contact between official medicine and folk medicine has resulted in conflict, however. Many folk-medicine practices have been acknowledged by official medical authorities as having genuine medicinal properties. Evidence of this can be found today. Acupuncture is one example. Practised for centuries in Eastern cultures, it is slowly being accepted by many Western "scientific" medical practitioners.

Folk Medicine and Christianity

In some senses, the folk healer is both a medical and spiritual healer. The relationship between official religion and folk healing is similar to the relationship between official medicine and folk healing. Even if many members of the laity have respected the folk healers, leaders of the Christian churches have generally been intolerant of other perceptions of the spiritual world. Folk healers have been officially seen as insubordinate to Christian teachings. In attempts to banish people's links with paganism, churchmen canvassed against wizards and witches and others who were believed to be engaged in magic. Witch-hunting was common from the fourteenth to seventeenth centuries across most of Europe.

"Witches represented a political, religious and sexual threat to the Protestant and Catholic churches alike, as well as to the state" (Ehrenreich 1973, 5–6). Thousands of executions, often by means of burning at the stake, were staged in Italy, Scotland, and other European countries. The victims were often accused of crimes that had to do with healing: "they [were] accused of having magical powers affecting health—of harming, but also of healing. They were often charged specifically with possessing medical and obstetrical skills" (Ehrenreich 1973, 8).

However, as was the case with official medicine, no force could simply obliterate centuries of pre-Christian tradition *in toto*. As a result, a syncretic belief system began to emerge, containing elements of both worldviews somewhat as a compromise. Slavic scholars call this phenomenon *dvoievir'ia* or "dual belief" (Ilarion 1965, 313–39; Tokarev 1957).

In some instances, saints' names replaced those of various pagan deities. "When heathenism was dethroned by Christianity, those ancient adjurations were so far altered, that for the names of the elementary deities were substituted those of the Saviour, the Virgin Mary, the Apostles, and various saints and martyrs" (Ralston [1872] 1970, 362). Some archaic incantations, for example, have been incorporated into Christian prayers: "there are instances in which, while the archaic form of the *zagovor* (incantation) is preserved, its tone has become to all appearance thoroughly Christian; so that it has even found its way under the heading *Molitvi*, or prayers, into the church books called *trebniki* (sacramentaries), both Russian and Serbian, of the 15th–17th centuries" (Ralston [1872] 1970, 363–4). For example:

> Forgive me, O Lord; forgive me, O Holy Mother of God; forgive me, O ye Angels, Archangels, Cherubim and Seraphim, and all ye Heavenly Host! Forgive, O Sky; forgive, O damp-mother-earth; forgive, O Sun; forgive, O Moon; forgive, ye Stars; forgive, ye Lakes, ye Rivers and Hills; forgive, all ye Heavenly and Earthly Elements! (Ralston [1872] 1970, 365)

Afanas'ev gives another example of an incantation that combines Christian and pagan elements. Here the conjurer intones a prayer against a snake bite:

> Zaklynaiu vas, hadiuky, imenem Hospoda nasheho Isusa Khrysta i sv. Heorhiia i vsimy nebesnymy sylamy.[4] (Afanas'ev [1865–9]1970, 40)

Kemp (1935, 110) notes that South Slavic peasants seldom have separate words for church prayers and exorcisms or healing formulas. It is evident, therefore, that the people have ingeniously evolved a symbiotic medical system that not only allows for but respects an intricate balance of magical and scientific worldviews.

---

4. I conjure you, snakes, in the name of our Lord Jesus Christ and St. George and all the heavenly forces.

Elements of the Wax Ceremony

Incantation

Humankind has long believed in the supernatural power of the word (Alexander 1975, 113; Boltarovych 1980, 95; Kolessa [1938] 1983, 30–5). The puissance of the word is very well known not only in magico-religious folk medicine, but in other genres of folklore as well, curses and blessings for example (Samuels 1970). The prayer used by the folk healer wields power and even medicinal properties in the mind of the patient. The formula or incantation is one of the tools used by the healer to intercede between deity and patient.

The incantation is indeed a powerful tool for healing. In the wax ceremony, the incantation, though often kept secret and uttered inaudibly, is an integral part of the healing process. In the minds of many patients and healers, the ceremony would have no effect without an accompanying incantation.

Water

Like the word, water has often been credited with magical qualities. Water is an ancient symbol. For centuries it has been used as an agent in healing.

The use of water for cleansing and purification is reflected in various Slavic customs and calendrical celebrations. Dew collected during the morning of the Feast of St. George (6 May N.S.), was considered to have medicinal properties. People gathered dew before the sun rose on this feast day. Those who had fallen ill would wash their eyes with the magical dew; adults would wash their heads to prevent headaches; and young maidens would wet themselves with the dew so they would be beautiful (Voropai 1958–66, 2: 69). Similarly, water was believed to have healing and magical properties during the eve of the feast of Kupalo (St. John the Baptist, 7 July). Water drunk on the eve of Kupalo was believed to be especially powerful (Boltarovych 1980, 101–2).

Ralston writes that disease was driven away "by purification with fire and water, and so the popular practice of physics is founded on a theory of fumigations, washings, and sprinklings attended by exorcisms of various kinds" ([1872] 1970, 379–80).

The magical and medicinal qualities attributed to water are related to its uses in washing. By extension, water can wash away sickness or evil. This is evident in the following incantation:

Vodychko-Iordanychko,
Umyvaiesh luhy-berehy, korinnia, bile kaminnia,
Umyi seho rshchenoho, chysto vrodzhenoho,
Vid ubrodu, hnivu, nenavysti i vid usiakoho zloho.[5]
(Boltarovych 1980, 99)

In parts of Ukraine, water was considered "the best medicine." Its value was appreciated both when poured over the afflicted area and when given to the patient to drink (Domanyts'kyi 1905, 100). Rainwater, in particular, was believed to have special curative powers (Afanas'ev [1865–9] 1970, 364). One way to say "it is raining" in Ukrainian is "doshch ide"—" the rain is going," rather than just falling out of the sky. Some scholars perceive this as a form of personification reflecting its high regard (Ilarion 1965, 40–3). Spitting and defecating in water were forbidden (Chubinskii 1872, 1: 42, Vovk [1928] 1976, 171). Water has been prayed upon, blessed, and used in various Christian rituals, illustrating a significant degree of influence and perhaps compatibility with folk practice (Shumovs'kyi 1955, 19–21).

In Ukrainian folk tradition, as in other Slavic cultures, water is often classified as either *mertva voda* (lifeless water) or *zhyva voda* (living water). *Mertva voda* is water from a still source—a pond or a well, for example. *Zhyva voda* is water taken from a running stream or river. Ralston discusses references to *mertva voda* and *zhyva voda* in Slavic magical tales: "But they [Slavic tales] differ from most of the similar stories in this respect. They have two species of what is called the 'strong' or the 'heroic' water. The one is called 'the dead water' (*mertvaya voda*); the other the 'living [or vivifying] water' (*zhivaya*

5. O water of the Jordan,
You wash the meadows and the banks, the roots, the white rock,
Cleanse this baptized, blamelessly born one
From excesses, sin, hatred, and from all evil.

voda). When the 'dead water' is applied to the wounds of a corpse it heals them, but before the dead body can be brought to life, it is necessary to sprinkle it with the 'living water'" ([1872] 1970, 97).

Living water is considered most potent for healing and magic. A Christianized remnant of this practice consists of adding a few drops of holy water to healing water (Shumovs'kyi 1955, 19–21). This practice has been noted among the healers who perform the wax ceremony in Alberta.

Water that has been used for cleansing or some purification ritual is poured onto the ground well away from paths where people might travel. If a human treads on that area, illness or discontent may be transferred (Boltarovych 1980, 106).

In Slavic folk medicine, water has been used both in divination and diagnosis ceremonies. Hydromancy (divination by means of water) has been commonly practiced by Slavic folk healers in an attempt to peer into the future. Among the Macedonians, an incantation was uttered while hot molten lead was dropped into water. The congealed forms were then interpreted and the future was told. A similar practice, using molten lead, eggs, or molten wax, was performed by Russians on Christmas Eve or New Year's Eve (Abbott 1903, 52; Miroliubov 1982, 159–60). A similar practice has been documented in Hungary (Dömötör 1982, 204).

Wax

Wax is an important element in Ukrainian folk rituals. Its special symbolism is related to its production by bees, sometimes affectionately called "God's birds" or "God's flies" (Ilarion 1965, 50). Beekeeping has a long history in Ukraine, where wax and honey have historically been important commodities (Onats'kyi 1957; Borovsky 1984). In a dualistic worldview, wax may be seen as holy because it is used in church candles. Certainly, blessed candles are used in a variety of folk customs and rituals (Ilarion 1965, 50; Voropai 1958–66, 1: 198; Onats'kyi 1964; Kylymnyk 1963, 5: 168–70).

Shukhevych reports several cures that involved beeswax in the Hutsul region of western Ukraine, and several lengthy incantations that accompanied these cures (1908, 215, 219–21, 242–50). Wax has been used in healing rituals in other Slavic groups as well (Kemp 1935, 17, 132–5).

Wax was also widely used as an agent of witchcraft and fortune-telling in Ukrainian culture. In one example similar to voodoo, wax dolls were made depicting an enemy and were poked with a needle or thrown into a fire (Onats'kyi 1957).

But wax is not the only substance to be used in Slavic healing rituals. The use of lead, solder, and eggs has also been documented (Kemp 1935, 55, 131–3, 135; Mealing 1972, 38). Wax, lead, and solder all have a relatively low melting temperature and can be poured into cold water to solidify. Beeswax, eggs, solder, and lead have also been known as curative agents in other cultures.[6] Coals were sometimes cast on water as a cure for the evil eye (Lepkii 1884, 106; Shukhevych 1908, 246–7).

A Ukrainian ceremony in which an egg was used to cure fear has been documented. A *babka* rolled an egg over a patient's body and then broke it into water. The cure was said to be guaranteed if the healer was able to discern the cause of a fear by interpreting the egg-white formations (Podolinskii 1879, 186). In other descriptions, an egg was rolled over an inflicted person and then thrown to dogs to eat (Chubinskii 1872, 42, 131). The same practice was described by informants for this study (Interview 23, 153; Interview 25, 157; Interview 18, 120–1).

Divination

There are many descriptions of the use of wax in fortune-telling in Ukrainian and other Slavic folklore. One tradition consisted of mixing a baby's hair with melted wax. If this nugget of wax and hair floated in a container of water, the child would have a long life. If it sank, the opposite was foretold (Afanas'ev [1865–9] 1970, 192–4).

In most descriptions, melted wax is poured into cold water. Fortune-telling rituals are often alluded to in nineteenth-century Ukrainian poetry, such as in the works of Levko Borovykovs'kyi and Taras Shevchenko.

---

6. Madsen and Madsen describe how a Mexican *currandero* exorcises cave air or evil spirits from a patient by rubbing him with an egg, which is then broken into a glass of water; the illness is diagnosed from the egg-white formations (1972, 28, 37). Dorson describes how Illinois Egyptians applied a woolen cloth dipped in beeswax and other substances to the thorax to cure respiratory infections (1964, 325). Thompson describes the medieval English belief in making an offering of a candle to St. Blaise, a martyr associated with throat disorders, to alleviate the pain of a toothache (1946, 170).

...Visk topyly na zharku
I z vodoiu v cherepku
Doliu vylyvaly...[7]

(Borovykovs'kyi, [1829] 1971, 21)

I vorozhka vorozhyla,
Prystrit zamovliala,
Talan-Doliu za try shahy
Z vosku vylyvala.[8]

(Shevchenko, quoted in Ilarion 1965, 200)

Nechui-Viter's short story "Ne bulo zmalku—ne bude i dostanku" contains a lengthy dialogue between a young girl and a fortune-teller, who, by reading the waxen figures, is able to tell the girl that she should soon prepare herself for a suitor (1861, 23–4). The scholarly and literary evidence about the use of wax in fortune-telling is corroborated by the field research done for this study.[9]

Using divination to cure illness is a very old form of medicine. Kemp (1935, 184) writes about its power and diagnostic function: "Diagnosis can effect a cure: it is part of and sometimes the whole of a treatment. All therapeutic rites include an act of identification, and generally an intention to define and to diagnose, but sometimes it is this that seems to be the main content, and to be more significant than the initial purpose.... This is clear in methods of water divining with lead or wax or hot coals, etc."

7. ...They melted wax over a flame,
And with water in a clay vessel,
They poured forth their fate...

8. And the soothsayer prophesied,
Charming the Evil Eye,
For three coins
Pouring destiny and fortune from the wax.

9. One of the informants, Mrs. A. R., described how she pours wax as part of fortune-telling. Because she is quite well known, she sometimes pours wax for this purpose several times a month.

The divinatory process is clearly evident in the wax ceremony. Accompanying incantations, actions, and tools are centred around the divining. This process affords the healer a glimpse into the soul and body of the patient. The goals are a diagnosis and resultant cure.

Faith

The wax ceremony, like other folk medicines, relies heavily on the faith of the patient. The more the patient believes in the power of the healer, the greater is the likelihood of a successful cure.

Healers and their patients have a symbiotic relationship. The patient depends on the healer for a cure; the healer in turn depends on her or his own success and the trust of this patient to attract other patients. The higher the success rate of healers, the better known and more valued they become. As more patients seek their services, their reputation, status, and income increase. Income may be in the form of money or goods. As a healer develops a following, the clientele's faith is strengthened. "[The healer] is not content only to activate the faith of the patient, but also instills in the whole group a certain conviction of the success of his treatment, awakens the collective faith and promotes the integration of the group. The system of social values as a whole supports his activities, the myths, the religious dogmas, the group feeling of solidarity and the patterns of role-behaviour" (Honko 1964, 352–4).

This interdependency applies to folk healers and physicians alike. For healers to be effective, it is essential that they believe in themselves and what they are doing. It has been noted that healers are able to influence the belief of patients by their mannerisms and what they say ("Chary" 1961, 129). If the healers are confident, their patients will be confident as well.

Fear Sickness

Although the wax ceremony is said to cure many different maladies, it is most commonly used as a cure for fear. In the culture of the informants, untreated fear is thought to manifest itself in emotional and mental illness. The informants identify general unhappiness or having an overall bad feeling as other signs of fear. They also say that physical problems such as weak kidneys (resulting in bed-wetting among children), speech impediments (such as stuttering), tremor, and epilepsy are also caused by fear sickness.

Informants claimed that the wax ceremony was able to cure a long list of symptom-specific maladies: sleepwalking (Mr. V. M. [Interview 18, 121–2]); nightmares (Mr. E. B. [Interview 8, 42–4]); talking in one's sleep (Mr. V. M. [Interview 18, 121–2]); insomnia (Mrs. S. K. [Interview 9, 53]); restlessness (Mrs. S. K. [Interview 9, 54]); bedwetting (Mr. E. B. [Interview 8, 42–4]); incessant crying (Mrs. V. J. [Interview 17, 111]); heart attacks (Mrs. H. K. [Interview 4, 17]); high blood pressure (Mrs. H. K. [Interview 4, 16]); epilepsy (Mrs. O. H. [Interview 26, 169]); failing memory (Mrs. H. B. [Interview 25, 163]); hiccups (Mrs. H. B. [Interview 25, 158–9]); poor study habits (Mrs. H. B. [Interview 25, 158–9], Mrs. S. K. [Interview 9, 53]); loss of appetite (Mrs. S. K. [Interview 9, 53]); lack of concentration (Mrs. S. K. [Interview 9, 53]); stomach gas (Mrs. H. B. [Interview 25, 164]); poor comprehension (Mrs. S. K. [Interview 9, 55]); crankiness (Mrs. S. K. [Interview 9, 55]); frothing at the mouth (Mrs. V. B. [Interview 5, 26]); car sickness (Mrs. S. N. [Interview 22, 149]); headaches (Mrs. S. N. [Interview 22, 149], Mrs. D. M. [Interview 27, 170]); marriage problems (Mrs. J. T. [Interview 11, 73]); and birthmarks (Mrs. S. B. [Interview 16, 96]). Some also believed that supernatural phenomena such as witchcraft and the evil eye could be counteracted by the wax ceremony (Mrs. D. M. [Interview 27, 170]; Mrs. J. T. [Interview 11, 73]).

The informants agreed that fear sickness becomes more threatening if it is not dealt with immediately. Mrs. K. W. always keeps a supply of holy water on hand. She administers it to her grandson as soon as he becomes frightened by something. She takes his fear very seriously and gives him the water so that the fear does not settle in during the night—"*aby ne zaspalo*" (Mrs. K. W. [Interview 15, 87]). Once a patient is repeatedly allowed to sleep with his or her fears, the sickness is believed to be compounded. The term used by the informants to express this phenomenon of compounded fear is "*strakh zadavnenyi*," that is, "fear that has been left alone to settle in." Although it is possible to cure this type of fear sickness, informants believed it would often take more than one wax pouring to accomplish the task (Mrs. J. T. [Interview 11, 73]; Mrs. M. H. [Interview 13, 79]; Mrs. S. K. [Interview 9, 54]; Mrs. K. W. [Interview 15, 85]).

Pain and Illness Transference

Many cultures have shared the belief that it is possible to transfer illness to other people or to animals. Before the understanding of germs became widespread, the transference of illness was perceived as an unnatural event. Pain and illness, for example, were often seen as being cast by an evil glance. Among Ukrainians in Alberta, the wax ceremony has been a culturally significant way of getting rid of the evil eye, which is still feared by many people, especially of the older generation.

During the wax ceremony, the pain is removed or flushed out from the body. It is transferred to an inanimate intermediary, water or wax. This is most clear in those cases where the water is discarded in some place where nobody will ever walk. This practice reduces the chances of illness being transferred to some unfortunate person.[10]

10. See the discussion of water above. In other cases, the healers give the water to the patient to take home and bathe in or drink. The concept of illness transference to the water is clearly not important in the minds of the healers in these cases. The water remains holy and retains healing properties. Perhaps they perceive that the illness is transferred to the wax or is in the water or wax only temporarily.

The Wax Ceremony

For this study, seven wax healers were interviewed or observed while pouring wax. Six were practicing their medicine in 1986.[11] Each healer's method and tools were unique yet similar.

Mr. P. G.

When Ms. D. N. (who volunteered to be a patient) and I arrived for our appointment with Mr. P. G., we had to wait in his kitchen. There were two other people in this makeshift waiting room; some magazines were on the small coffee table. Mr. P. G.'s wife chatted with us while making chicken soup. The phone rang several times during our wait. Mr. P. G.'s wife answered the calls and arranged appointments by marking the callers' names on a wall calendar. Throughout the house dozens of Roman Catholic statuettes and Byzantine icons were displayed. Newspapers were strewn about the kitchen floor to protect it from the dirt brought in by the constant traffic of patients. The actual healing ceremony took place in two other rooms of the house. One small room contained a bed covered in white sheets. Here Mr. P. G. set bones and did massages. Across the hall, in another room, he poured wax and performed fumigations.

A small amount of salt and holy water were sprinkled into an enamel bowl containing water. Mr. P. G. asked Ms. D. N. what her symptoms were. Both of them faced east throughout the proceedings. Before pouring, Mr. P. G. crossed himself three times. All three times that he poured wax, he did so behind the patient while holding the bowl over her head. During the first pouring he held a butter knife and the bowl in his right hand. He also held a hair comb in his right hand during the second pouring. During the third pouring he added a stone. Mr. P. G. did not read or interpret the wax figures. Before each pouring, he recited an inaudible incantation, apparently in English.

After the pouring, Mr. P. G. made the sign of the cross across the top of the patient's head and down the entire length of her hair. Then he

11. Since then, Mrs. V. B. and Mrs. M. H. have passed away.

pressed his hands firmly to her temples, washed the back of her neck and her cheeks, and, one at a time, immersed and washed her hands in the water.

After the washing, Mr. P. G. took a metal cup with a candlesticklike socket and church incense in it, and proceeded to fumigate the patient. He began at her head and walked around her chair counterclockwise. Upon completing the fumigation, the healer told Ms. D. N. not to lend or borrow anything for the next three days. He cautioned her that if she did, the wax ceremony would be rendered ineffectual. Mr. P. G. then said that his fee was ten dollars, which Ms. D. N. left on a table. He did not pick up the money in our presence. As we were leaving, he repeated several times that the patient would feel better and that she was not to worry anymore. Mr. P. G. appeared hurried throughout the pouring. When we left, there were other patients waiting to see him.

Mrs. J. T.

Of the seven healers, Mrs. J. T. had the broadest definition of what the wax ceremony could cure. Her style of pouring incorporated several unique practices. She used the wax ceremony for fortune-telling and for healing fear sickness.

Mrs. J. T. poured wax in the middle of her kitchen. She kept her implements on a small table in that room. The patient (Ms. D. N.) and I visited her before noon on a Saturday. Mrs. J. T. greeted us warmly and served us coffee and sweets. After talking with the patient for about an hour and ascertaining that she was troubled by nervous tension, Mrs. J. T. busied herself melting wax and preparing her implements for the pouring. She spent a half hour relaxing and talking to Ms. D. N. after she had performed the ceremony.

The patient was asked to sit facing west while the healer faced east. The healer crossed herself three times and then uttered an inaudible incantation over the patient's head while holding a plastic bowl of water.[12] In the bowl, holy water had been added to the tap water just before the commencement of the ceremony. Mrs. J. T. held a blunt knife

12. Mrs. J. T. was not willing to "give up" her entire incantation for fear of losing her power to heal, but she did recite parts of it to me.

in her right hand as she worked. Just before she poured the wax, she asked Ms. D. N. to make a wish.

Once the poured wax had congealed, Mrs. J. T. read both sides of it. In addition to diagnosing the source of the patient's nervous tension, she told her fortune and read her palms. She spent a good deal of time talking to the patient about the absence of a mate in the patient's life. As she was reading the wax, she reassured Ms. D. N. many times that troubling issues in her life would be resolved and things would work out.

Upon completion of the treatment, a square, white face cloth was meticulously folded into a smaller, perfect square by pulling all four corners of the cloth towards the centre. In a counterclockwise direction, Mrs. J. T. washed the face and hands of the patient with the cloth.

Immediately after the washing, the patient was asked to sip the water. The remaining water was poured into an empty mayonnaise jar and given to the patient to take home. The patient was instructed to wash her face and hands with the water for three consecutive nights before retiring. On the first and second evenings, she was to use a cloth folded like the facecloth at the healing. Ms. D. N. was to make a wish before washing and then wash on the first two evenings using an inward motion ("*do sebe*"). On the third evening she was to wish to get rid of something while washing with an outward motion ("*vid sebe*"). Any excess water was to be disposed of immediately by throwing it away from the body under a tree or somewhere where it was impossible for a human to walk.

No fee was mentioned by Mrs. J. T. When the patient left ten dollars, she was assured that half of the money would be donated to the local Ukrainian church. Mrs. J. T. did not pick up the money in the presence of the patient or the researcher.

Mrs. S. K.

After contacting Mrs. S. K. on several occasions, the researcher was invited to her house to discuss the wax ceremony. Mrs. S. K. would not agree to be watched while treating an actual patient. She said that it would not be proper for her to be observed in action.

Mrs. S. K. is a devout Catholic, and she had several crosses, icons, and holy books about her house. She told the researcher that she performed the ceremony in her living room or in her kitchen.

Mrs. S. K. preferred to pour wax on Tuesdays, Wednesdays, and Thursdays: she had been told by her mother that the days in the middle of the week were better for pouring. If possible, she poured before noon. She said that the patient was not as tired in the morning and thus could concentrate better.

Mrs. S. K. said that when she performed the wax ceremony, the patient sat opposite her. No preferred direction was indicated. Mrs. S. K. said she began the ceremony by crossing herself three times and then making the sign of the cross over a bowl of water with her fingers. The patient was asked to look into the water, and Mrs. S. K. then lifted the bowl over the patient's head and poured molten beeswax into the water. She also said that she recited the Lord's Prayer before the patient arrived. She said that while the wax was hardening, she talked to her patients.

Mrs. S. K. said that she spent about half an hour with each patient. If patients wanted to know what the wax had revealed, she would show them and would discuss it with them. Otherwise, she did not interpret the congealed shapes.

Mrs. S. K. said that after a healing session she might serve refreshments. She said she always emptied the water that had been used during the session onto a plant or somewhere where people could not walk. She never disposed of the "diseased" water in the sink lest a human come in contact with it. She did not normally accept money or gifts in return for her services. On one occasion, however, she accepted a gift from a cousin because she felt it would make him feel better.

Mrs. K. W.

Mrs. K. W. claimed to have performed the wax ceremony only a few times in her life. She too thought it better not to have the researcher observe her in action, but spoke very openly about her healing. This healer performed the ceremony only for her family. She refused to treat strangers because she said that anybody who wanted to could learn to pour wax.

Mrs. K. W. said that she poured wax in her own home when her children and grandchildren came for help. She did so in her kitchen, a room filled with Ukrainian decal pottery trinkets.

Mrs. K. W. had a fairly negative attitude towards other wax healers. She had been disillusioned by a healer who charged thirty dollars per treatment. Mrs. K. W. said she felt that this healer was only out to make money.

Mrs. K. W. claimed to have learned wax pouring from a healer who had been born in the same Ukrainian village as she. The first few times she poured wax, she adhered to a fairly stringent routine, but circumstances had forced some adaptations over the years. For example, Mrs. K. W. had been taught to draw water from a well before sunrise. In the city she was forced to take water from a tap, but she nevertheless did so before sunrise on the day that she was to pour wax. She added some holy water to the tap water for "extra strength."

When Mrs. K. W. conducted the wax ceremony, she asked her patient to face west, while she herself faced east. She began by crossing herself three times and reciting the Lord's Prayer in Ukrainian.

Mrs. K. W. said she poured wax nine times per treatment: three times over the head of the patient, three times at the chest of the patient, and three times at the back. She was careful to pour it away from herself. She held a knife in her right hand during the pouring because the knife severed the fear from the patient—"*nozhem vidtenaiese strakh.*" Mrs. K. W. did not know how to interpret the congealed wax figures, so as soon as the wax had set she remelted it.

After the wax had been poured nine times, Mrs. K. W. washed her patient's hands and face in a counterclockwise direction. When the washing was completed, she disposed of the wax and water in the kitchen sink.

Mrs. M. H.

Mrs. M. H. usually poured wax in the kitchen of her rural home. She occasionally made house calls if patients were disabled or too ill to come to her. Several icons, to which she made frequent reference, adorned the room where she poured wax.

On two separate occasions when the researcher and patient (Ms. D. N.) arrived at Mrs. M. H.'s home, an elaborate lunch of several courses of Ukrainian food was served. Mrs. M. H. had prepared herself for wax pouring: a small, black, cast-iron frying pan containing a lump of beeswax was set off to the side of the stove. An enamel bowl, a towel, and a small jar of water marked with a cross were placed on her counter.

One of two known healers in a small town in Alberta, Mrs. M. H. said that she received so many requests for the wax ceremony that it was difficult for her to keep up. She said that women could come to her for pourings on Wednesdays and Fridays, while men could come on Mondays, Tuesdays, and Thursdays. Mrs. M. H. did not pour wax on Saturdays or Sundays.

The patient was asked to sit facing east. Before beginning, Mrs. M. H. recited a quiet prayer over a bowl of water to which some holy water had been added. She then used this water to wash her hands and a butter knife that was to be used in the ceremony. She made the sign of the cross over the water, and with her right hand she poured the wax towards herself while holding the bowl above the head of the patient. After the wax had congealed, Mrs. M. H. interpreted its shapes. This process was repeated three times. At the conclusion of the third pouring, which was identical to the first two, Mrs. M. H. said that the patient would have to return as the fear was compounded ("*strakh zadavnenyi*"): it had been with the patient for quite some time.

The second session that the patient had with Mrs. M. H. consisted of seven pourings, all following the pattern described above. After the seventh pouring the healer was finally satisfied that the patient had been totally exorcised of the evil that had been cast upon her.

At the conclusion of each of the two sessions, the patient was asked to wash her own hands and face. The healer immediately disposed of the water by throwing it on the snow under a tree. Mrs. M. H. claimed that while she had no special incantation other than the Lord's Prayer, she added the words: "*Ty Bozhe pomozhy meni nyni to, shcho ia robiu*" (God, help me today with what I am doing).

Ten dollars were left for Mrs. M. H. at the conclusion of each of the two sessions. The healer said that she did not charge for her work, but since the patient had given her money, she in turn would donate it to the local church. Mrs. M. H. did not pick up the money in the presence of the researcher or the patient.

Mrs. D. M.

Mrs. D. M. poured wax in her home. At each visit, she was careful to draw the attention of the researcher to her collection of numerous religious icons and books, family photo albums, and Ukrainian handicrafts such as embroidery and Easter eggs. Mrs. D. M. was very proud of her Ukrainian heritage.

After chatting with her patient, Mrs. D. M. filled a large bowl with tap water. Beeswax was melted in a small container on the stove. Mrs. D. M. explained that a teaspoon tucked under a belt or in a brassiere would keep fear sickness from being transferred to her. The spoon had to be worn with its bowl facing outward, away from the healer.

Mrs. D. M. began the wax ceremony by crossing herself three times and reciting a prayer. She faced east while her patient sat facing west. She held a butter knife in her right hand and made the sign of the cross over the water. The first pouring was done over the head of the patient. A second pouring was done at the chest of the patient. A third pouring was performed at the knees or calves of the patient. Each time, once the wax had congealed, Mrs. D. M. spent some time studying the shapes with her patient. If a shape was apparent ("*iasno*"), such as a bolt of lightning or a dog, Mrs. D. M. shared this knowledge with her patient. Mrs. D. M. claimed that in general she was unable to interpret the shapes.

After the third pouring, Mrs. D. M. washed the patient with her right hand, which she dipped in the water into which the wax had been poured. The face and hands of the patient were washed in a counterclockwise direction ("*na viglie*"). The patient was given the remaining water in a jar and instructed to add the "blessed" water to his bathwater on the evening of the day on which the wax had been poured. If the patient was an infant, the mother was to bathe the child in the water. If the patient was an adult, he was told to sponge bathe using the water and then dispose of it at a crossroad or water a dry plant, tree, or shrub with it. A human foot could never make contact with the water.

At the end of all four interviews, Mrs. D. M. served tea, coffee, and pastry. Before her visitors had left, she would not pick up the money that they had left for her. She explained that the money would be donated to her church, because her work was not her own but that of God.

Mrs. D. M. preferred to pour wax on Saturday. She had no special rules about what days of the week to pour wax, but she would not pour it on Sunday. She spent approximately one hour with each patient.

Mrs. V. B.

Of the seven healers interviewed for this study, Mrs. V. B. was the best known. She was extremely popular and sought after as a healer up until her death in 1986. Family members estimated that in some seventy-five years of her practice, more than 10,000 people had visited her from across Alberta, the rest of Canada, and the United States. Five of the six other healers interviewed for this study had either known Mrs. V. B. or heard of her. Two acknowledged having visited her as patients.

Mrs. V. B. was very humble about her healing. While she was very open to discussing her experiences of coming to Canada and pioneer life on the prairies, she was reluctant to share her knowledge of healing. Another researcher had interviewed Mrs. V. B. in 1971 while recording information about Ukrainian Canadian lifestyles. Mrs. V. B. told that researcher that she did not want to talk about the wax ceremony. But she had been willing to discuss herbal teas and other types of remedies of which she had knowledge.

I had to be extremely diplomatic and persistent in order to establish a special trust and rapport with Mrs. V. B. and to persuade her to discuss her skills and accomplishments as a healer. Initially Mrs. V. B.'s responses to my inquiries were vague and noncommittal. In this translated excerpt from an early interview, Mrs. V. B. suggests that the wax ceremony was nothing special:

> R. H. : Can you tell me your incantation?
> Mrs. V. B. : Well, there isn't very much to it at all . . . you have to cross yourself, and then you say, "God help me."
>
> (Interview 6, 29)

Eventually I established a special trust with Mrs. V. B. Indeed, she became the primary subject of this study. Family members had made audio recordings while she was performing the ceremony. She and family members allowed transcriptions of the incantations to be made.

I was even allowed to make a video recording while Mrs. V. B. poured wax for her grandson.

During her healing career, Mrs. V. B. had poured wax in a variety of locations. If a patient was too ill to visit her, she made house calls. Most of her healing was done while she lived with her son and his family. In the basement of her son's home Mrs. V. B. had an area equipped with a hot plate that was reserved for practicing her medicine. If more than one patient came to visit at one time or arrived early for their appointment, they were often asked to wait upstairs in the kitchen. If refreshments were offered after the wax pouring, they were served in the kitchen. The following description of Mrs. V. B.'s healing technique is synthesized from the three interviews I conducted with her.

Mrs. V. B. faced east, while patients were seated facing west. The healer asked her patients to place their feet flat on the ground and to rest their hands palms down in their laps.

If the patient was older than Mrs. V. B., she performed a special protective ritual before the wax ceremony. She rarely discussed this ritual. A description was offered by Mrs. V. B.'s granddaughter, who explained that it involved a special prayer that was chanted in a corner outside the room where the patient was seated (Mrs. V. J. [Interview 17, 111]). Mrs. V. B. kept a special amulet somewhere on her person in the event that she would be asked to pour wax for a patient who was her elder. Though family members were not clear as to where and how the amulet was worn, it appears that Mrs. V. B. sometimes wore a cloth amulet around her neck. The amulet was square and was filled with an unknown substance to protect Mrs. V. B. from transference of the sickness from the older patient to herself (Mrs. S. B. and Mrs. M. B. [Interview 16, 103–4]). If the patient was younger than Mrs. V. B., no amulet was required.

After the necessary precautions were taken, Mrs. V. B. prepared water and wax for the wax ceremony. She placed a single clove of garlic in cold water, which she drew from the tap, and added several generous drops of blessed water. She always put the water in a white enamel bowl. Mrs. V. B. prepared beeswax by melting it in a white enamel cup. To it she added some paraffin wax shavings from a candle that had been blessed in an Easter basket (Mrs. N. D. and Mrs. M. K. [Interview 28,

180]). She talked to her patients while she prepared the water and implements. Everything from the patient's symptoms to general family news was discussed.

When the water and wax were ready, Mrs. V. B. stood in front of her patient. She crossed herself three times, reciting the trinitarian formula invoking the Father, the Son, and the Holy Spirit. She then recited a lengthy incantation while holding a butter knife and the water bowl over the head of the patient. After her incantation, she poured the melted wax into the bowl, which she still held over the patient's head.

Mrs. V. B. paid great attention to the interpretation of wax shapes. She shared her interpretations with the patient. Once she had interpreted as much as she believed was possible, she returned the wax to the enamel cup and reheated it. She repeated the incantation with a few appropriate variations at the patient's chest, and performed a third pouring behind the patient, holding her bowl and cup at the patient's shoulders. Again, the incantation incorporated variations appropriate to the location at which the pouring was being made.

After each pouring, Mrs. V. B. used her knife to make the sign of the cross over her patient. At the first pouring the sign was made over the patient's head. At the second pouring it was made over the chest, and at the third pouring, down the length of the head and back and across the shoulders.

After the third pouring Mrs. V. B. took a small shot glass, filled it with the water in which the wax had congealed, and gave it to the patient to drink. The patient was instructed to drink the water in three small sips.

After the patient had drunk the water, Mrs. V. B. used the back of her hand and the remaining water to wash the face, hands, and feet of the patient. If the patient was an infant, the accompanying adult was then given the water to take home so that it could be added to the child's bathwater. If the patient was an adult, Mrs. V. B. poured the water outside under a spruce tree or watered a house plant with it after the patient left.

Illustration 1. Mrs. V. B.'s healing instruments, from the top clockwise. White enamel bowl into which molten wax is poured; it contains tap and holy water and one clove of garlic. White enamel cup in which wax is melted. Metal-and-plastic butter knife. Incenser. Shot glass from which the patient drinks.

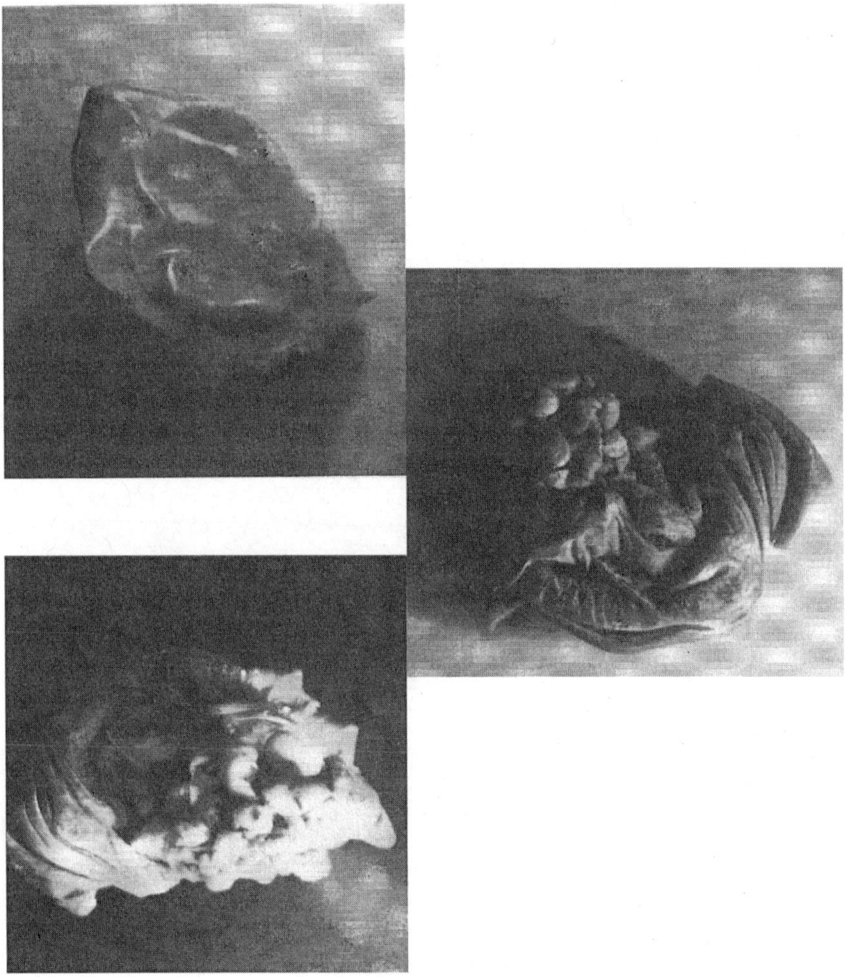

Illustration 2. Wax shapes. (Top) Smooth surface of hardened wax indicating a patient's fears have been alleviated or totally "poured out." (Middle) Two pointed protrusions, lower left quadrant, indicating a patient has been frightened by a loud or sudden noise. Ripples in the wax, upper right quadrant, indicating the patient has been frightened by water. (Bottom) Curly, clumped protrusions, lower right quadrant, indicating bad nerves. Ripples in wax, bottom left quadrant, indicating the patient has been frightened by water.

Table 1. Healer Profile

Healer	P. G.	J. T.	S. K.	K. W.	M. H.	D. M.	V. B.
Age	60+	69	50+	74	70	90	93
Sex	M	F	F	F	F	F	F
Place of Birth	Canada	Alberta	Alberta	Kysiliv village, Chernivtsi oblast', Ukraine	L'viv, Ukraine	Bila village, Chernivtsi oblast', Ukraine	Banyliv village, Vashkivtsi county, Ukraine
Emigration to Canada	—	—	—	1926	1949	1902	c 1898
Parents' Place of Birth	Unknown	Unknown	F-r: Sniatyn, Ukraine. M-r: Leduc, Alberta	As above	As above	As above	As above
Occupation	Farmer	Housewife	Housewife	Housewife	Housewife	Housewife	Housewife
Healing Teacher	Unknown	Mrs S, local "Old Country" healer	Mother	Mrs W, local healer from Andrew, Alberta	Aunt in Ukraine	Mother	Mother-in-law from Borivtsi, Ukraine
Location	Vegreville	Mundare	Edmonton	Edmonton	Mundare	Edmonton	Edmonton
Years of Prac-tice	Unknown	30+	25	Unknown	40+	75+	75+
No. of Patients	200+	1,000+	40+	10+	Unknown	20+	10,000+
Religion	Unknown	Ukr Orth.	Ukr Cath.	Ukr Orth.	Ukr Orth.	Ukr Orth.	Ukr Orth.
Nat. Lang.	English (?)	Ukrainian	English	Ukrainian	Ukrainian	Ukrainian	Ukrainian
Marital Status	Married	Widowed	Widowed	Widowed	Widowed	Widowed	Widowed
Pass on Practice?	Unknown	Yes, to 3 persons	Yes	Unknown	No intentions	Yes	Yes

Before the water was disposed of, the piece of garlic was removed, wrapped in a paper towel, and given to the patient to take home. The patient was to wear the garlic "close to the heart." Informants said that they could wear the clove in an armpit or a brassiere until they retired that evening. The garlic was then to be placed under the patient's pillow. The patient was not to discard the garlic: it should eventually disappear "on its own," without specific action by the patient.

After the washing, Mrs. V. B. fumigated her patient with a bundle made from special ribbons wrapped tightly around unidentified, locally grown herbs and grasses. The ribbons had originally been used at church to mark pages in the Gospel. They had been acquired in exchange for newly bought ribbons that Mrs. V. B. supplied to her priest. The entire bundle was dipped in beeswax to prevent it from burning too quickly. As indicated in the glossary of this study, the bundle was referred to as "*sviachenne*" or "*pidkuriuvalo*" by Mrs. V. B.'s family.

At the conclusion of the session, money could be left for Mrs. V. B. at the discretion of the patient. The patient was assured that there was no set price for Mrs. V. B.'s healing services. If he or she wished to leave a payment, the money would be donated to the Church.

Mrs. V. B. spent approximately forty-five minutes to one hour with each patient. She was aware of designated female and male healing days of the week, but because she was so much in demand, she accommodated her patients whenever she could. She did not perform healings on Sundays, church holidays, or a few days before a new moon, known as empty days ("*porozhni dni*").

A Comparison of Healing Techniques

Time. Almost all of the healers had prescribed days and times when they would pour wax. While none of them would pour wax on a Sunday, Mrs. J. T., Mrs. S. K., and Mrs. D. M. preferred to pour wax on Saturday. Mr. P. G. and Mrs. V. B. poured wax whenever they had time, except on Sundays. Mrs. V. B. would not pour on special saint's days or on "empty days," which she explained were the last three or four days of the fourth quarter of the moon. Such restrictions are evident in other Ukrainian folk medical rituals. For example, the noted Ukrainian ethnographer Khvedir Vovk refers to heavy days ("*tiazhki dni*") on which healing is not well executed ([1928] 1976, 167).

All the healers had either heard of or were currently adhering to men's days or women's days. In order to be most effective, men and women should come only on days reserved for them. No two healers agreed, however, on which days were best for which gender.

Place and Direction. Most of the healers interviewed for this study performed the wax ceremony in the kitchens of their homes. Mr. P. G. had a special room that he used only for this purpose. Mrs. V. B. poured wax in a special room in her basement. While each of the healers had a preferred location for pouring wax, they agreed that the ceremony could be performed anywhere.

Six of the seven healers took orientation into account before beginning to work. Either they or their patients faced east. North or south orientations were never prescribed.

The penchant for ritual directions that is common in folk medicine can perhaps be explained by an association with and dependence upon the firmaments—the sun, the moon, and the stars. Celestial bodies rise in the east, and Christians have traditionally viewed the east as sacred. Eastern Christian churches, for example, are traditionally built so that worshippers and the priest face east. This is whence Christ will return at the second coming. The tradition of turning towards the east before praying is documented worldwide. Peasants in the Russian Empire in the last century believed that people who had taken ill must face east in order to be cured of their maladies (Ralston [1872] 1970, 360).

With the exception of Mrs. S. K., all of the healers believed that the water used in the wax ceremony was to be discarded in a direction away from the body. Five of the healers believed that the washing of body parts was to be performed counterclockwise. The exception was Mrs. V. B., who washed the face, hands, and feet of her patients clockwise. Mr. P. G. fumigated patients by walking around them counterclockwise. Mrs. J. T. instructed her patients to wash counterclockwise for the first two nights after the wax ceremony had been performed. On the third night they were to wash clockwise. The use of a counterclockwise or counter-sunwise direction has been explained as a reversal or return to the better (Hand 1980, 4). The sickness, the evil, and the fear must be

Table 2. Healing Techniques: A Comparison of Healers

Healer	P. G.	J. T.	S. K.	K. W.	M. H.	D. M.	V. B.
Direction	East	East	No Pref.	East	East	East	East
Time water drawn	Any time	Anytime	Anytime	Before sunrise	Anytime	Any time	Anytime
Healing Day	Most	Sat.	Tues., Thurs.	Any	Women: Wed Fri. Men: Mon Tues Thur	Sat.	Most
Healing Time	Any time	Before noon	Before noon	Anytime	Before noon	Anytime	Anytime
Healer Crosses Self	Yes	Yes	Yes	Yes	No	Yes	Yes
Healer Prays	Yes	Yes	Yes	Yes	Yes	Yes	Yes
No. of Pourings	3	1	1	9	3+	3	3
Washing	Yes	Yes	No	Yes	Yes	Yes	Yes
Drinking	No	Yes	No	No	No	No	Yes
Insufflation	No	No	No	No	No	No	Yes
Fumigating	Yes	No	No	No	No	No	Yes
Interpreting	No	Yes	Some	No	Yes	Some	Yes
Payment	$10	Not set	None	None	Not set	Not set	Not set
Special instructions	Do not lend or borrow anything for 3 days	Make wish while washing towards and away from self for 3 nights	None	None	None	Bathe with water	Take garlic home and sleep on it

removed, and harmony must be restored: the negative situation must be "countered" or reversed.

Medical Materials. All of the healers used beeswax, which they purchased at the Ukrainian Bookstore in Edmonton. Occasionally they would receive beeswax as gifts or payment from patients who had access to beehives.

Mrs. V. B. incorporated several items that she considered holy into her healing: a candle that had been blessed in her Easter basket, ribbons that were used as bookmarks in the priest's service book, and old altar cloths. The curative significance of priests' vestments or other items from church has been documented in ethnographic literature on eastern Europe (Red'ko 1899, 80). In the popular mind the power that these items wield is commensurate with the frequency with which they are handled by the priest.

While Mrs. V. B. was the only healer who used garlic during the wax ceremony, several others told the researcher that they had heard of this practice. Mrs. V. B. was a firm believer in the power of garlic not only to cure when ingested, but to protect from evil. Garlic has long been used in eastern Europe to ward off sickness. After a woman gave birth, a clove of garlic was placed under her pillow to protect her and the newborn child from evil spirits (Red'ko 1899, 60, 83).

Mr. P. G. was the only healer who added salt to his bowl of water before beginning the wax ceremony. The use of salt in folk medicine is not uncommon. It was well known in Russia for keeping evil spirits away from new mothers or pregnant women; hot coals and salt were put into water and prayed over in a divinatory process to cure restlessness and general feelings of agitation (Dmitriukov 1831, 367).

All of the healers held a butter knife in the right hand while performing the wax ceremony. They explained that the knife was important because it "cut fear away" from the patient. Some of them asserted that the knife needed to have a smooth edge so that the life of the patient would continue smoothly after the ceremony had been performed (Mrs. V. J. [Interview 17, 112]). In Ukrainian tradition, a knife was given to pregnant women to protect them from evil and sickness; the knife was tucked under their pillows and slept on (Red'ko 1899, 82).

Mr. P. G. used a comb as part of his ritual when pouring wax, saying that the comb would "comb away" fear from the patient.[13]

Each of the healers had a favourite set of utensils that they used exclusively for the wax ceremony and for no other purpose. Enamel cups for melting wax and enamel bowls for the water seemed to be the most popular with the healers. Mrs. M. H. and Mrs. D. M. used black cast-iron frying pans to melt beeswax.

Protective Talismans. Mrs. V. B. and Mrs. D. M. strongly believed that it was necessary to protect themselves from the translocation of sickness. Mrs. V. B. wore a special square, cloth amulet and recited a prayer outside the room when she was healing a patient older than herself. Mrs. D. M. wore a spoon, with its bowl facing outward, in her belt or brassiere.

Mrs. S. K. said she had to pray and be at peace with herself and God before beginning the wax ceremony. The other four healers indicated no special preparatory process, though all but one of the healers crossed themselves three times before pouring wax.

Water. Mrs. M. H., who resided in a rural location, still used water drawn from a well. Mrs. S. K., K. W., D. M., and V. B. all preferred water from a natural source such as a well, but they only had easy access to tap water. With the exception of Mrs. K. W., none of the healers indicated a preferred time to draw water. Mrs. K. W. drew her water before sunrise on the day she was to pour wax. Mrs. V. B., Mr. P. G., and Mrs. J. T. added a few drops of holy water, which they got from their church, to the healing water.

Mrs. V. B. and Mrs. J. T. were the only healers who consistently ended the wax ceremony by asking their patients to take home the water into which they had poured the molten wax. Other healers poured the water under a plant or down the sink.

---

13. A comb was also used in a Scottish cure for sore breasts. It and a pair of scissors were placed into a sieve in a form of a cross, and water and melted lead were slowly poured over them. The hardened lead shapes were then examined by the healer to see if any of the formations resembled a heart (Black 1970, 90).

Incantation. Immediately after crossing themselves at the beginning of the wax ceremony, the healers prayed to God, to saints, to the Mother of God, and sometimes to other intercessors, such as the stars or the moon. Mr. P. G. and Mrs. S. K. apparently prayed in English. The remaining five healers recited their prayers in Ukrainian. Mrs. V. B. and Mrs. D. M. recited their opening incantations aloud. All of the other incantations were whispered over the head of the patient or were totally inaudible.

Mrs. V. B. was the only healer who said she had to steal the words to her incantations from her mother-in-law. All of the other healers learned them from family members or other healers.

Number of Pourings. For the most part, the healers poured wax in threes or multiples of three. Two healers, Mrs. J. T. and Mrs. S. K., poured wax one time per visit. Though Mrs. M. H. generally poured wax three times, sometimes repeating the process as many times as necessary for the wax to solidify with a smooth surface and thereby indicate a cure. During one visit she poured wax seven times. More commonly, Mrs. M. H. and various other healers asked their patients to return if the wax did not come out smooth after a third pouring. Alternatively, patients might decide to return for another pouring if they felt their symptoms had not totally subsided.

Reading the Wax Shapes. Four out of the seven healers tried to discern figures in the congealed wax formations. Mrs. V. B. spent the most time interpreting or reading the shapes. Mrs. J. T. read both sides of the wax and also used the shapes to predict the future for her patients. Mrs. D. M. said she would tell her patient what she saw if she found very obvious configurations in the wax; however, she claimed not to be well versed in interpretation. Mrs. S. K. did not talk about what she could discern in the wax unless she was specifically requested to do so by her patient.

Washing. All of the healers, with the exception of Mrs. S. K., washed their patients' face and hands after performing the wax ceremony. Mrs. V. B. also washed the feet of her patients. Mrs. J. T. had an elaborate system of folding the washcloth that she used to wash the patient.

Table 3. Medical Materials: A Comparison of Healers

Healer	P. G.	J. T.	S. K.	K. W.	M. H.	D. M.	V. B.
Water Source	Tap	Tap	Tap	Tap	Well	Tap	Tap
Holy Water	No	Yes	No	Yes	Yes	No	Yes
Holy Candles	No	No	No	No	No	No	Yes
Beeswax	Yes	Yes	Yes	Yes	Yes	Yes	Yes
Garlic	No	No	No	No	No	No	Yes
Salt	Yes	No	No	No	No	No	No
Knife	Yes	Yes	Yes	Yes	Yes	Yes	Yes
Comb	Yes	No	No	No	No	No	No
Rock	Yes	No	No	No	No	No	No
Protective Talisman	No	No	No	No	No	Teaspoon in belt	Cloth amulet
Vessels	Enamel cup, bowl	Plastic bowl, cup	Enamel bowl	?	Plastic bowl, pan	Bowl, pan	Enamel bowl, cup

Fumigation and Insufflation. Mr. P. G. and Mrs. V. B. were the only healers who fumigated or incensed their patients during the wax ceremony. They both fumigated around the patient in a counterclockwise direction. While Mrs. V. B. used church ribbons wrapped around a bundle of herbs, Mr. P. G. burned church incense in a metal cup. After fumigating, Mrs. V. B. rubbed ashes on the patient's hands and forehead. Drazheva writes that Russians and Ukrainians traditionally burned grasses to ward off various sicknesses. Both the patient and the dwelling were incensed. Belarusians fumigated in order to ward off the evil eye and to dispel fear (Drazheva 1973, 114). "The people … had spatial conceptions of natural processes as coming and going … if the person who was ill was enveloped in smoke, it was done to induce the illness to go out of him" (Petrov 1963, 343).

Mrs. V. B. was the only healer to blow evil and sickness away from her patients. This ancient act retains a place in Christian worship both in the Ukrainian church and in other churches: insufflation symbolizes the expulsion of evil while conferring the Holy Spirit.

Instructions. Four out of seven healers sent their patients home with very specific instructions. Mr. P. G. told his patients not to lend anything out of the household for three days after the wax pouring. Mrs. J. T. told her patients to arrange a facecloth into a smaller square by folding all four corners towards the middle of the cloth. Mrs. D. M. instructed her patients to wash or sponge-bathe with the water from the wax ceremony. Mrs. V. B. sent her patients home with the garlic that had been placed in the water, instructing them to sleep on it until they lost track of the garlic.

Fees. With the exception of Mr. P. G., none of the healers set a fee for their services. Mr. P. G. asked for ten dollars per visit. The other healers indicated that a portion or all of the money left by their patients would be given to a church of the healer's choosing. None of the healers directly took the payment in his or her hands. It was incumbent upon the patient to leave the offering in a conspicuous place.

Other Healing Rituals for Fear Sickness

While the wax ceremony is the most popular remedy in the treatment of fear sickness, other methods have also been used. One method involves fumigating the patient. If the source of the affliction is known, the hair, feathers, fur, or clothing of the culprit is taken or stolen and set on fire, and the patient is asked to inhale the smoke. Unlike the wax ceremony, this method of healing apparently does not require a special sage. It appears that anyone except the patient is able to perform this ritual.

Informants provided the following examples of fumigation used to cure fear sickness. Mrs. H. B. said that she has made her son inhale smoke from turkey feathers that she set on fire because her son had been frightened by the bird. She also explained that a woman she knows took some fur from a cat that had frightened a child, and burned it to fumigate the child. If a human has frightened someone, Mrs. H. B. said it was necessary to get some of the offending person's hair and burn it (Interview 25, 163). Mr. B. B. described how his wife burned some hair from a cow that had frightened their son in order to rid him of fear (Interview 10, 64). When Mrs. D. M. was asked whether such fumigations or the wax ceremony proved more successful in expelling fear from the body, she replied that both were equally useful (Interview 27, 179).

Another known remedy for expelling fear, particularly fear that has been caused by the evil eye, is to wash the face of the patient with urine. "Washing oneself in one's own urine ... can usually put an end to suffering caused by the 'evil eye'" (Klymasz 1980, 65). This belief was corroborated by several informants interviewed for this study. Mr. R. B. claimed that if one of his sons became afflicted with the evil eye, he or his wife would wipe the child's face with a wet diaper. He said this helped to "wipe him into a relaxed state." (Interview 7, 38–9). Mrs. H. B. said that she washed her son with her own urine after the child had the evil eye cast upon him. She said she washed his entire body, paying particular attention to the heart area of the chest because it is most vulnerable to the evil eye (Interview 25, 162).

Incantations

An incantation is a prayer uttered by the specialized diviner or healer at a specific time in a specific place in a predetermined manner that is apropos to the entire act.

The wax ceremony is never performed without accompanying words. All seven healers had a formula that was an integral part of their healing. These words are referred to as *molytva* (prayer), *slova* (words), *prymivka/prymovka*, *zamovlennia/zamovliannia*, *zachytuvannia*, *zaklynannia*, and *zahovor* (incantation).

Mrs. V. B.

Of the documented incantations used by the healers interviewed for this study, Mrs. V. B.'s prayers were the most extensive. She used six different incantations during the wax ceremony and a seventh one for other healing rituals. The basic formula for the first three incantations was the same. Mrs. V. B. enlisted the aid of higher powers to effect the healing, and then in the name of these powers she exorcised the evil to places where no human would ever go. Once removed from the body, the evil was commanded to stay away and to cause no further harm to the patient.

Incantation One. This incantation removes evil from the head, blood, and all the joints of the patient. It is intoned over the head of the patient while a knife is held in the right hand and an enamel bowl, into which molten wax is poured, is held in the left hand.

1 Berúsia do [im'ia] holový, do [im'ia] króvy, do [im'ia] usíkh sustavók,
2 Vyzyváty, vyklykáty tsei strákh strakhovýi,
3 Opívnishnyi, polúdnishnyi,[14]

---

14. 1 I take to the head of [name], to the blood of [name], to all the joints of [name].
2 To adjure, to summon this fear of fears,
3 From the north and from the south,

4 Z okhóty, z robóty, z ïdý, z vodý,
5 Náslanyi, záspanyi.
6 Ia z lykhým chysóm vyzyváiu,
7 Vyklykáiu ne samá sobóiu, a Hóspodom
8 Bóhom Isúsom Khrystóm i z Mátir Bózhov
9 I sestrýtsi-zirnýtsi
10 Ie vas simdesiát sím i odná,
11 Dopomaháite my khodýty, dopomaháite my robýty,
12 Pomozhít [im'ia] tsei strákh zastanovýty.
13 [Im'ia] sy z tsým ne rodýv, [im'ia] sy z tsým ne khrystýv,
14 [Im'ia] sy z tsým ne myruváv.
15 Shchezái i propadái vid [im'ia] holový, vid [im'ia] krový,
16 Vid [im'ia] usíkh sustavók.
17 Chervónu króv ne pýi, bíle kílo ne sushý, zhóvtu kíst' ne lupái,
18 Kólo sértsia ne uvielý,
19 Hnizdó sobí ne robý.
20 Ia tebé vyzyváiu Bózhymy hubámy, Bózhymy slovámy,
21 Za hóry, za móre vidpuskáiu.
22 Budésh ty hóramy perevertáty,[15]

15. 4 From want, from work, from food, from water,
5 Sent upon us, steeped in sleep.
6 With the evil hour I adjure you,
7 I summon you not by my power alone, but by the power of the Lord
8 God Jesus Christ with the Mother of God
9 And the sister-stars—
10 You number seventy-seven and one.
11 Help me to walk, help me to work,
12 Help [name] to contain this fear.
13 [Name] was not born with this, [name] was not baptized with this,
14 [Name] was not anointed with this.
15 Disappear and vanish from [name's] head, from [name's] blood,
16 From all [name's] joints.
17 Do not drink red blood, dehydrate a white body, or strip a yellow bone
18 By the heart do not appear,
19 Do not make yourself a nest.
20 I summon you with God's lips, with God's words,
21 And release you beyond the mountains, beyond the seas.
22 There you will turn over mountains,

23 Piskámy peresypáty, vódamy perelyváty, lisámy lomáty.
24 By [im'ia] spáv, spochyváv, léhku ních mav,
25 Za tsei strákh ne znáv.
26 Ia tebé kósamy vykósuvaiu, serpámy vyzhynáiu,
27 Na zelíznim tukú rozbyváiu.
28 Vohón' pohoríie, pópil popelíie.
29 Shchezái i propadái vid [im'ia] holový, vid [im'ia] krový, vid [im'ia] usíkh sustavók.
30 Ia tebé zastanovýla Bózhymy hubámy, Bózhymy slovámy,
31 Iak zastanovýv Hóspod' sorokodénnyi na nébi i na zemlý,
32 Tak zastanovýv, [im'ia] tsiu króv
33 Zaliúshchu, paliúshchu,
34 Zavedéno, ubrydéno, náslano, záspano.
35 Z okhóty, z robóty, z ïdý, z vodý, z vorókiv, zo skókiv.
36 Ia tebé zastanovýla, zasumorýla,
37 Za hóry, za móre vidpustýla,
38 Tam de liúdy ne khódut,
39 De kúry ne píiut,
40 De víter ne víie,[16]

---

16. 23 Pour over sands, pour over waters, and break forests.
24 Let [name] sleep, rest, and have a easy night,
25 And no longer know of this fear.
26 I cut you down with scythes, with sickles I mow you down,
27 On a steel anvil I break you apart.
28 The fire will burn down, and the ashes will turn to dust.
29 Disappear and vanish from [name's] head, from [name's] blood, from all the joints of [name].
30 I have arrested you with God's lips, with God's words,
31 As the Lord did after forty days in heaven and on earth,
32 So He arrested [name's] blood,
33 Burning and hot,
34 As was instigated, putrified, sent upon us, steeped in sleep.
35 From desire, from work, from food, from water, from the Evil Eye, from jumps
36 I have arrested you, mortified you,
37 Released you beyond the mountains, beyond the seas,
38 Where people do not walk,
39 Where roosters do not crow,
40 Where the wind does not blow,

41 De sóntse ne hríie.
42 Tam tobí huliáty,
43 Tam tobí nochuváty,
44 Tam tobí rozkoshuváty,
45 Tam tobí hnizdó máty.
46 By [im'ia] spáv, vidpochyváv,
47 Léhku ních mav, za tsei strákh ne znáv.
48 Shchezái i propadái vid [im'ia] holový, vid [im'ia] krový,
49 Vid [im'ia] usíkh sustavók.
50 Ia tebé vyzyváiu z mózku, z-pid mózku,
51 Z cholá, z-pid cholá,
52 Z brív, z-pid brív,
53 Z ochéi, z-pid ochéi,
54 Z hubéi, z-pid hubéi,
55 Zo zubéi, z-pid zubéi,
56 Z borodý, z-pid borodý,
57 Z shýï, z-pid shýï,
58 Z sértsia, z pid sértsia,
59 Z pechinók, z-pid pechinók,[17]

17. 41 Where the sun does not warm.
42 That is where you are to play.
43 That is where you are to spend the night.
44 That is where you are to luxuriate.
45 That is where you shall have your nest.
46 Let [name] sleep, rest,
47 And have a peaceful night, not knowing this fear [any longer].
48 Disappear and vanish from [name's] head, from [name's] blood,
49 From all the joints of [name].
50 I summon you from the brain, from under the brain,
51 From the forehead, from under the forehead,
52 From the brows, from under the brows,
53 From the eyes, from under the eyes,
54 From the lips, from under the lips,
55 From the teeth, from under the teeth,
56 From the chin, from under the chin,
57 From the neck, from under the neck,
58 From the heart, from under the heart,
59 From the viscera, from under the viscera,

60 Z slyzanók, z-pid slyzanók,
61 Vid usíkh sustavók.
62 Ia tebé vyzyváiu, nozhámy roztynáiu.
63 Shchezái i propadái vid [im'ia] holový, vid [im'ia] sértsia,
64 Vid [im'ia] pechinók, vid usíkh sustavók.
65 Chervónu króv ne pýi, bíle kílo ne sushý, zhóvtu kíst' ne lupái,
66 Kólo sértsia ne uvielý,
67 Hnizdó sobí ne robý.
68 Shchezái i propadái.
69 Vid méne prymóva, vid Bóha falós.
70 Vid méne prymóva, vid Bóha falós.
71 Vid Bóha vík, a vid méne lík.
72 I ne chesnók, ne vohón', sam Hóspod' rozbói.
73 I ne chesnók, ne vohón', sam Hóspod' rozbói.
74 I ne chesnók, ne vohón', sam Hóspod' rozbói.
[Wax is poured into the water and the incantation continues]
75 Zastanovýty, zasumorýty
76 Tsiu króv zaliúshchu, paliúshchu,
77 Zavedéno, ubrydéno,
78 Náslano, záspano.[18]

---

18. 60 From the spleen, from under the spleen,
61 From all the joints.
62 I adjure you, with knives cut you apart.
63 Disappear and vanish from [name's] head, from [name's] heart,
64 From [name's] viscera, from all of the joints.
65 Do not drink red blood, dehydrate a white body, strip a yellow bone,
66 By the heart do not appear,
67 Do not make yourself a nest.
68 Disappear and vanish.
69 I say the incantation, from God in His voice.
70 I say the incantation, from God in His voice.
71 God gives life, while I give the cure.
72–4 It is not the garlic, not the fire, the Lord Himself is doing battle. [3X]
[Wax is poured into the water and the incantation continues]
75 To arrest, to mortify
76 This blood that is burning and hot,
77 As was instigated, putrified,
78 Sent upon us, steeped in sleep.

Incantation Two. This incantation is very similar in style and form to Incantation One. Intoned in front of the patient at the chest, it serves to exorcise the heart, viscera, and spleen.

Incantations One and Two do not differ except in lines 1, 15, 29, and 48, where the head and blood in Incantation One are replaced with the heart, and viscera. Lines 50–62, where evil is being pulled from the top of the brain down to the spleen, are unique to Incantation One. Consequently the second incantation is shorter than the first.

1 Berúsia do [im'ia] sértsia, do [im'ia] pechinók, do [im'ia] slyzanók,
2 Vyzyváty, vyklykáty tsei strákh strakhovýi,
3 Opívnishnyi, polúdnishnyi,
4 Z okhóty, z robóty, z ïdý, z vodý,
5 Náslanyi, záspanyi.
6 Ia z lykhým chysóm vyzyváiu,
7 Vyklykáiu ne samá sobóiu, a Hóspodom
8 Bóhom Isúsom Khrystóm i z Mátir Bózhov
9 I sestrýtsi-zirnýtsi
10 Ie vas simdesiát sím i odná,
11 Dopomaháite my khodýty, dopomaháite my robýty,
12 Pomozhít [im'ia] tsei strákh zastanovýty.
13 [Im'ia] sy z tsým ne rodýv, [im'ia], sy z tsým ne khrystýv,
14 [Im'ia] sy z tsým ne myruváv.
15 Shchezái i propadái vid [im'ia] sértsia, vid [im'ia] pechinók,
16 Vid [im'ia] usíkh sustavók.
17 Chervónu króv ne pýi, bíle kílo ne sushý, zhóvtu kíst' ne lupái,
18 Kólo sértsia ne uvielý,
19 Hnizdó sobí ne robý.
20 Ia tebé vyzyváiu Bózhymy hubámy, Bózhymy slovámy,
21 Za hóry, za móre vidpuskáiu.
22 Budésh ty hóramy perevertáty,
23 Piskámy peresypáty, vódamy perelyváty, lisámy lomáty.
24 By [im'ia] spáv, spochyváv, léhku ních mav,
25 Za tsei strákh ne znáv.
26 Ia tebé kósamy vykósuvaiu, serpámy vyzhynáiu,

27 Na zelíznim tukú rozbyváiu.
28 Vohón' pohoríie, pópil popelíie.
29 Shchezái i propadái vid [im'ia] sértsia, vid [im'ia] pechinók,
vid [im'ia] usíkh sustavók.
30 Ia tebé zastanovýla Bózhymy hubámy, Bózhymy slovámy,
31 Iak zastanovýv Hóspod' sorokodénnyi na nébi i na zemlý,
32 Tak zastanovýv, [im'ia] tsiu króv
33 Zaliúshchu, paliúshchu,
34 Zavedéno, ubrydéno, náslano, záspano.
35 Z okhóty, z robóty, z ïdý, z vodý, z vorókiv, zo skókiv.
36 Ia tebé zastanovýla, zasumorýla,
37 Za hóry, za móre vidpustýla,
38 Tam de liúdy ne khódut,
39 De kúry ne piiút,
40 De víter ne víie,
41 De sóntse ne hríie.
42 Tam tobí huliáty,
43 Tam tobí nochuváty,
44 Tam tobí rozkoshuváty,
45 Tam tobí hnizdó máty,
46 By [im'ia] spáv, vidpochyváv,
47 Léhku ních mav, za tsei strákh ne znáv.
48 Shchezái i propadái vid [im'ia] sértsia, vid [im'ia] pechinók,
49 Vid [im'ia] usíkh slyzanók.*
50 Chervónu króv ne pýi, bíle kílo ne sushý, zhóvtu kíst' ne lupái,
51 Kólo sértsia ne uvielý,
52 Hnizdó sobí ne robý.
53 Shchezái i propadái.
54 Vid méne promóva, vid Bóha falós.
55 Vid méne promóva, vid Bóha falós.
56 Vid Bóha vík, a vid méne lík.
57 I ne chesnók, ne vohón', sam Hóspod' rozbói.
58 I ne chesnók, ne vohón', sam Hóspod' rozbói.
59 I ne chesnók, ne vohón', sam Hóspod' rozbói.
[Wax is poured into the water and the incantation continues]
60 Zastanovýty, zasumorýty

61 Tsiu króv zaliúshchu, paliúshchu,
62 Zavedéno, ubrydéno,
63 Náslano, záspano.

Incantation Three. This incantation is almost identical to Incantation One. Intoned behind the patient at shoulder level, it exorcises evil from the upper back, the lower back, and all the joints. The incantation is the same as Incantation Two except that the heart, viscera, and spleen have been replaced by the upper back, lower back, and joints in lines 1, 15–16, and 29. Lines 48–49 refer to body parts contained in Incantations One, Two, and Three.

1 Berúsia do [im'ia] plechéi, do [im'ia] kryzhéi, do [im'ia] usíkh sustavók,
2 Vyzyváty, vyklykáty tsei strákh strakhovýi,
3 Opívnishnyi, polúdnishnyi,
4 Z okhóty, z robóty, z ïdý, z vodý,
5 Náslanyi, záspanyi.
6 Ia z lykhým chysóm vyzyváiu,
7 Vyklykáiu ne samá sobóiu, a Hóspodom
8 Bóhom Isúsom Khrystóm i z Mátir Bózhov
9 I sestrýtsi-zirnýtsi
10 Ie vas simdesiát sím i odná,
11 Dopomaháite my khodýty, dopomaháite my robýty,
12 Pomozhít [im'ia] tsei strákh zastanovýty.
13 [Im'ia] sy z tsým ne rodýv, [im'ia] sy z tsým ne khrystýv,
14 [Im'ia] sy z tsým ne myruváv.
15 Shchezái i propadái vid [im'ia] plechéi, vid [im'ia] kryzhéi,
16 Vid usíkh sustavók.
17 Chervónu króv ne pýi, bíle kílo ne sushý, zhóvtu kíst' ne lupái,
18 Kólo sértsia ne uvielý,
19 Hnizdó sobí ne robý.
20 Ia tebé vyzyváiu Bózhymy hubámy, Bózhymy slovámy,
21 Za hóry, za móre vidpuskáiu.
22 Budésh ty hóramy perevertáty,
23 Piskámy peresypáty, vódamy perelyváty, lisámy lomáty.

24 By [im'ia] spáv, spochyváv, léhku ních mav,
25 Za tsei strákh ne znáv.
26 Ia tebé kósamy vykósuvaiu, serpámy vyzhynáiu,
27 Na zelíznim tukú rozbyváiu.
28 Vohón' pohoríie, pópil popelíie.
29 Shchezái i propadái vid [im'ia] plechéi, vid [im'ia] kryzhéi, vid [im'ia] usíkh sustavók.
30 Ia tebé zastanovýla Bózhymy hubámy, Bózhymy slovámy,
31 Iak zastanovýv Hóspod' sorokodénnyi na nébi i na zemlý,
32 Tak zastanovýv, [im'ia] tsiu króv
33 Zaliúshchu, paliúshchu,
34 Zavedéno, ubrydéno, náslano, záspano.
35 Z okhóty, z robóty, z ïdý, z vodý, z vorókiv, zo skókiv.
36 Ia tebé zastanovýla, zasumorýla,
37 Za hóry, za móre vidpustýla,
38 Tam de liúdy ne khódut,
39 De kúry ne píiut,
40 De víter ne víie,
41 De sóntse ne hríie.
42 Tam tobí huliáty,
43 Tam tobí nochuváty,
44 Tam tobí rozkoshuváty,
45 Tam tobí hnizdó máty.
46 By [im'ia] spáv, vidpochyváv,
47 Léhku ních mav, za tsei strákh ne znáv.
48 Shchezái i propadái vid [im'ia] holový, vid [im'ia] sértsia, vid [im'ia] pechinók, vid [im'ia] plechéi, vid [im'ia] kryzhéi,
49 Vid usíkh sustavók.
50 Shchezái i propadái.
51 Vid méne prymóva, vid Bóha falós.
52 Vid méne prymóva, vid Bóha falós.
53 Vid Bóha vík, a vid méne lík.
54 I ne chesnók, ne vohón', sam Hóspod' rozbói.
55 I ne chesnók, ne vohón', sam Hóspod' rozbói.
56 I ne chesnók, ne vohón', sam Hóspod' rozbói.
[Wax is poured into the water and the incantation continues]

57 Zastanovýty, zasumorýty
58 Tsiu króv zaliúshchu, paliúshchu
59 Zavedéno, ubrydéno,
60 Náslano, záspano.

Incantation Four. This incantation was intoned while Mrs. V. B. lightly washed the face, hands, chest, and feet of the patient. It involves sympathetic magic. As the water from the River Jordan washes clean the meadows and shores, so the curative water washes the patient clean from fear, horror, sickness, hatred, and bad nerves.

1 Tse vodá Iordána, do vs'óho prydána,
2 Mýie luhý, berehý.
3 Umyí vid tsého strakhú, vid tsého zhekhú,
4 Vid tséï slábosty, vid tséï nenávysty, vid tsykh nérviv.
5 Umyi vid tsého strakhú, vid tsého zhekhú,
6 Vid tséï slábosty, vid tséï nenávysty, vid tsykh nérviv.
7 Umýi vid tsého strakhú, vid tsého zhekhú,
8 Vid tséï slábosty, vid tséï nenávysty, vid tsykh nérviv.
9 Vid méne prymóva, vid Bóha falós.
10 Vid méne prymóva, vid Bóha falós.
11 Vid Bóha vík, a vid méne lík.[19]

19. 1 This is water of the Jordan: to everything it has use.
2 It washes the meadows and the shores.
3 Cleanse from this fear, from this horror,
4 From this sickness, from this hatred, from these nerves.
5 Cleanse from this fear, from this horror,
6 From this sickness, from this hatred, from these nerves.
7 Cleanse from this fear, from this horror,
8 From this sickness, from this hatred, from these nerves.
9 I say the incantation, from God in His voice.
10 I say the incantation, from God in His voice.
11 God gives life, while I give the cure.

Incantation Five. Mrs. V. B. fumigated her patients at the end of the wax ceremony. This incantation was intoned while a homemade censer, made out of ribbons tightly wound together, was burned to fumigate the patient. As in Incantation Four, imitative magic is at work. As the smoke rises and disappears over the Earth, so too shall the fear, sickness, hatred, and bad nerves that have plagued the patient.

1 Iak tsei dým sy rozkhódyt po svíti,
2 Tak by vid [im'ia] tsei strakh, tsia slábist',
3 Tse nenávist', tsi nérvy rozishlý sy. [3X] [20]

Incantation Six. This incantation was intoned while Mrs. V. B. insufflated the patient. The insufflation was performed over the top of the patient's head and around the face and back of the head in a counterclockwise direction.

1 Ia ne zduváiu pórokh, ále strákh.
2 Ia ne zduváiu pórokh, ále strákh i slábist'.
3 Ia ne zduváiu pórokh, ále strákh, slábist', nenávist', nérvy, uróky.
4 Shchezáty, propadáty vid [im'ia] holový, vid [im'ia] sértsia,
5 Vid [im'ia] pechinók, vid [im'ia] plechéi,
6 Vid [im'ia] kryzhéi, vid usíkh sustavók.
7 Chervónu krov ne pýi, bíle kílo ne sushý, zhóvtu kíst' ne lupái,[21]

20. 1 As this smoke disperses over the earth,
2 May from [name] this fear, this sickness,
3 This hatred, these nerves, disperse. [3X]

21. 1 I am not blowing away dust, but fear.
2 I am not blowing away dust, but fear and sickness.
3 I am not blowing away dust, but fear, sickness, hatred, nerves, and the Evil Eye.
4 To disappear and vanish from [name's] head, from [name's] heart,
5 From [name's] viscera, from [name's] upper back,
6 From [name's] lower back, from all the joints.
7 Do not drink red blood, dehydrate a white body, or strip a yellow bone

8 Kólo sértsia ne uvielý,
9 Hnizdó sobí ne robý.
10 Shchyzái i propadái na shchéstie, na zdoróvlie.[22]

Incantation Seven. This incantation was discovered after Mrs. V. B.'s death and forwarded to the researcher by Mrs. V. B.'s daughter. It was used to exorcise evil and sickness, but to the best of Mrs. V. B.'s family's knowledge, it was not used in conjunction with the wax ceremony. The form of this incantation parallels Incantation One of the wax ceremony. In both cases, the evil is commanded to leave various body parts, beginning with the skull and brain and ending with the blood.[23]

1 Mísiatsiu novyí, kníaziu molodyí,
2 Pishlý cholovíka na Osiiáns'ku horú.
3 U chervónim ubranniú ne idý tudá.
4 Ozmý daléko nozhív i prystupý do [im'ia]
5 I vyrubái satanú z holový
6 I výzhyny na hóry, na piský, na vódy.
7 Zaberý satanú z vólosu, z-pid vólosu,
8 Z shkíry, z-pid shkíry,
9 Z zhýliv, z-pid zhýliv,[24]

---

22. 8 By the heart do not appear
9 Do not make yourself a nest.
10 Disappear and be gone in the name of good fortune, of health.

23. The words in this incantation appear as they were pronounced by Mrs. V. B.'s daughter, Mrs. N. D.

24. 1 O, new moon, young prince,
2 Send a man to the Radiant [?] Mountain.
3 In red clothes you are not to go there.
4 Take the knives far away, and approach [name]
5 And cut out Satan from the head
6 And cast him out to the mountains, to the sands, to the waters.
7 Take Satan from the hair, from under the hair,
8 From the skin, from under the skin,
9 From the veins, from under the veins,

10 I z króvy.
11 Zaberý satanú,
12 Vidoshlý na hóry, na piský, na vódy i lyshít' [im'ia].
13 Zaberý satanú z chérepa, z-pid chérepa,
14 I z mózku,
15 I z cholá, z-pid cholá,
16 I bróvy,
17 I z ochéi, z-pid ochéi,
18 I lytsiá,
19 I z nósa, z-pid nósa,
20 I hubéi,
21 I z zubéi, z-pid zubéi,
22 I z iazyká,
23 I z hórla, z-pid hórla,
24 I z króvy.
25 Zaberý satanú,
26 Vidoshlý na hóry, na piský, na móre, na vódy.
27 Lyshít' [im'ia], iak i Máty na svít porodýla Tsár Bóha
28 I ochyshchý vid diiávola. [25]

---

25. 10 And from the blood.
11 Take Satan
12 Send him to the mountains, to the sands, to the waters, and let [name] alone.
13 Take Satan from the skull, from under the skull,
14 And from the brain,
15 And from the forehead, from under the forehead,
16 And [from] the brows,
17 And from the eyes, from under the eyes,
18 And from the face,
19 And from the nose, from under the nose,
20 And [from] the lips,
21 And from the teeth, from under the teeth,
22 And from the tongue,
23 And from the throat, and from under the throat,
24 And from the blood.
25 Take Satan
26 And send him to the mountains, to the sands, to the sea, to the waters.
27 Let [name] alone like the Mother brought the Lord God into the world.
28 And cleanse [him/her] from the devil.

29 Sóntse právedne,
30 Zishlý [im'ia] i Magdalýnu svoḯmy zolotýmy strúnamy[?]*
31 [Im'ia] zakladáv iomú [?] zolotýi strói sóntsia
32 U vólos, u shkíru, v zhýly, i v króv, i v chérep, i v mózok,
33 V choló, v bróvy, v óchi, v nís, v bórodu, v lytsé,
34 Dai vlást'
35 ______, ______* i vesélist' na kózhdim króku
36 Bud' chýsta, iak tebé máty na svít sotvorýla, vid ého zla.[26]

Mrs. S. K.

Mrs. S. K. chanted her one incantation entirely in English. With the exception of the last four lines, she recited the Lord's Prayer. She added her own personal touch by asking for Jesus' intercession in her healing.

1 Our Father, who art in Heaven,
2 Hallowed be Thy name.
3 Thy kingdom come,
4 Thy will be done
5 On Earth as it is in Heaven.
6 Give us this day our daily bread,
7 And forgive us our trespasses,
8 As we forgive those who trespass against us.
9 And lead us not into temptation,
10 But deliver us from evil.
11 For Thine is the Kingdom and the power and the glory, for ever and ever.

---

26. 29 True sun,
30 Send [name] and Magdalene with your golden rays [?]*
31 [Name] placed into him [?] the golden garb of the sun
32 Into the hair, the skin, the veins, the blood, the skull, and the brain,
33 The forehead, the brows, the eyes, the nose, the chin, the face,
34 Give power.
35 ______, ______[?]* and rejoice at every step.
36 Be pure as when your mother conceived you before this evil.

* unclear in the original, handwritten text.

12 Amen.
13 Help me as I will be pouring wax.
14 Help me, O Jesus, I pray with fear and love.
15 Just be with me and guide me,
16 And help me to remove the fear.

Mrs. D. M.

Mrs. D. M. used a total of three incantations. Like Mrs. V. B. and S. K., she prayed for intercession in her healing. After the afflicting fear was exorcised, it was commanded to go into roots, sands, banks, forests, and bodies of water.

Incantation One. This incantation was intoned over the head of the patient. Mrs. D. M. held a knife in her right hand and a bowl filled with water in her left hand.

1 Vo im'ia Otsá i Sýna i Sviatóho Dúkha, amín.
2 Vo im'ia Otsá i Sýna i Sviatóho Dúkha, amín.
3 Vo im'ia Otsá i Sýna i Sviatóho Dúkha, amín.
4 Ia prymívku promovliáiu ne samá sobóv, a z
5 Hóspodom Bóhom Isúsom Khrystóm z Mátir Bózhov.
6 Sviatýi Mykoláiu, ia strákh vidhoniáiu.
7 Tut tsému strakhóvy ne huliáty, tut iomú bíle tílo ne sushýty,
8 Krov ne spyváty, smért' ne zavdaváty.
9 Idý ty v korínnia, v piský, v berehý,
10 Na lisý, na vódy. [27]

27. 1 In the name of the Father, and the Son, and the Holy Spirit, Amen.
2 In the name of the Father, and the Son, and the Holy Spirit, Amen.
3 In the name of the Father, and the Son, and the Holy Spirit, Amen.
4 I recite this incantation not by myself, but with
5 The Lord God Jesus Christ and the Mother of God.
6 St. Nicholas, I am chasing away fear.
7 Here this fear should not revel, here it should not dehydrate a white body,
8 Drink blood, or impose death.
9 Go, you, to the roots, to the sands, to the banks,
10 To the forests, to the waters.

11 Dai spókyi [im'ia] shóby voná spála,
12 Spochyvála, vid Hóspoda Bóha vóliu mála.
13 Vid ména prymívka, vid Bóha sviatóho lík.
14 Nai tobí Boh pomaháie.[28]

Incantation Two. This incantation was intoned at the patient's chest. An exorcism sequence of numbers beginning with nine and ending at zero is an interesting feature.

1 Ia prymívku promovliáiu ne samá sobóv,
2 A z Hóspodom Bóhom Isúsom Khrystóm z Mátir Bózhov.
3 Sviatýi Mykoláiu, prymívku prymovliáiu.
4 Shóby ne málo mótsy horíty, bolíty, shuliáty, shpygáty.
5 Tsei strákh mav dévik strakhív,
6 Vív ïkh na dévik hotarív,
7 Zacháv ïkh rozsyláty pustýmy poliámy, krútymy doróhamy,
8 I z deviet'ókh sy lyshýlo visimókh,
9 Z visimókh, simókh,
10 Z simókh, shist'ókh,
11 Z shist'ókh, piet'ókh,
12 Z piet'ókh, shtyrókh,[29]

---

28. 11 Grant peace to [name] so that she may sleep,
12 Rest, and receive relief, from the Lord God.
13 I give the incantation, Holy God grants the cure.
14 May God help you.

29. 1 I utter this incantation not by myself alone ,
2 But with the Lord God Jesus Christ and the Mother of God.
3 St. Nicholas, I utter an incantation
4 So that it would not have the strength to burn, to hurt, to shoot pain, to stab.
5 This fear had nine fears,
6 And he led them to nine herds[?, perhaps hilltops. R. H.]
7 And he began to disperse them to empty fields, [onto] winding roads,
8 And from nine, eight remained.
9 And from eight, seven remained.
10 From seven, six.
11 From six, five.
12 From five, four.

13 Z shtyrókh, tr'okh,
14 Z tr'okh, dvokh,
15 Z dvokh, ne vodén.
16 Nai shchezáie, nai idé na lisý, na vódy,
17 I dast' spókii irshénii, porozhénii [im'ia]
18 Vid méne prymívka, a vid Bóha sviatóho lík.[30]

Incantation Three. This incantation was intoned at shoulder height behind the patient. It contains elements of imitative magic.

1 Ia prymovliáiu, ne samá sobóv,
2 A z Hóspodom Bóhom Isúsom Khrystóm z Mátir Bózhov.
3 Sviatýi Mykoláiu, ia strákh vidhoniáiu.
4 Shóby strákh ne mav mótsy horíty, bolíty, shuliáty, shpygáty
5 Bíle tílo ne sushýty, króv ne spyváty, smért' ne zavdaváty.
6 Idy ty na lisý, na vódy, na piský,
7 Rozidýsia, roztichýsia, iak na nébi khmára,
8 Na vohnévi vísk, a na vodí sil'
9 Vid [im'ia] irshénoï, porozhénoï,
10 Vid méne prymívka a vid Bóha sviatóho lík.[31]

---

30. 13 From four, three.
14 From three, two.
15 From two, not one.
16 May it disappear, may it go to the forests, to the waters,
17 And give peace to the baptized [and] born [name].
18 I give the incantation, Holy God grants the cure.

31. 1 I utter this incantation not by myself alone
2 But with the Lord Jesus Christ and the Mother of God.
3 St. Nicholas, I am chasing away fear.
4 So that the fear will not have strength to burn,to hurt, to shoot pain, to stab,
5 To dehydrate a white body, drink blood, or bring death.
6 Go, you, to the forests, to the waters, to the sands.
7 Disperse, dissipate like a cloud in the sky,
8 Wax on a flame, and salt on water,
9 From baptized [and] born [name].
10 I give the incantation, Holy God the cure.

Mrs. J. T.

Mrs. J. T. poured wax only once during a healing. She was unwilling to share her full incantation with me. I wrote down the following version of her incantation while I observed her pouring wax for a patient.

Ia ne samá sobóiu,
A Prechýsta Díva i Hóspod' Bóh
I vsi sviatí kotrí máiut sýla,
Peredái chérez móï rúky
V ímeni [im'ia] ta iohó/ïï nedúha
To nai idé sobí na lisý, hóry,
A iohó/ïï lýshut
[inaudible]
Za luhámy,
Piský peresypáty,
Vódy perelyváty
[inaudible][32]

---

32. I, not by my own power,
But with the power of the Virgin Mary and the Lord God
And all the saints who have powers,
Give [this power] through my hands
In the name of [name] and his/her infirmity
So let it go to the forests, the mountains,
And leave him/her alone
[inaudible]
Beyond the meadows,
To sift through sands,
And pour through waters
[inaudible]

General Features of the Incantations

According to Bronislaw Malinowski, incantations contain a formula that is comprised of three basic features: mythological allusion, invocation, and phonetic effect (1954, 73–4). Mythological allusions are intrinsic to almost every spell. According to Malinowski, they are references to ancestors or heroes that are expressed through various personae in the incantations. There are references to both Christian and non-Christian powers in the present material. The second element, invocation, is a type of command. The healer intrepidly threatens the malady with destruction using a command such as "I implore you to leave" or "I burn you as the sun burns." Phonetic effect is a formal characteristic of the text based on the frequency of certain significant sounds. We can identify several other formal features of incantations that merit attention: rhythm, repetition, symbolic numbers, and colours. Malinowski's categories have been adapted for the following discussion of (1) references to supernatural powers, (2) exorcism, and (3) the formal features of the texts.

References to Supernatural Powers. Before the four healers began their incantations, they crossed themselves three times and prayed, "In The Name of the Father, the Son, and the Holy Spirit." Mrs. D. M. incorporated the trinitarian formula directly into her incantation. The other three healers separated this action from the incantation proper.

The texts of the incantations include calls for the intercession of the Lord God, Jesus Christ, the Virgin Mary, the Mother of God, St. Nicholas, and all saints who have healing powers. All four healers asked for the power of God to work through them in order that they might effect a cure. Three of them added that while they were performing the ceremony, the cure itself came from God: "*Vid méne promóva, vid Bóha falós. Vid méne lik, a vid Bóha vik*" (From me the incantation, from God the voice. I give the cure, and God gives life).

Mrs. D. M. began her wax ceremony incantation by praying to St. Nicholas. It is common to find the names of saints in Slavic incantations. The following formula, recited to cure cataracts, also invokes this saint. The incantation is to be repeated three times. After each repetition, the healer spits in the eye(s) of the afflicted.

Ïkhav Sviatyi Mykolai na bilim koni
Do biloi tserkvy;
A v bilii tserkvi
Na bilim prestoli —
Presviataia Diva Mariia. (Bogdanovich 1877, 2: 278)[33]

St. Anthony is invoked in the following incantation to ward off a toothache:

Presviataia Bohorodytsia, prosym sobi v pomich.
Sviatyi otche Antoniiu, povrachuvav Hospodu-Bohu
Ot velykoï boleznosty, ot lomovoï kosty, ot semydesiat sustaviv,
Povrachui narozhdennomu, nakhreshchennomu [imrek],
Ot velykoï boleznosty, ot velykoï kosty, ot zuba.
Shchuka v mori, mii bat'ko vo hrobi.
Ot seï pory, u narozhdennoho, u khreshchenoho [imrek]
Zuby ne bolitymut'. [Spliun' 3 raza]. (Dragomanov 1876, 29)[34]

The Christian elements that are prominent in many Slavic incantations have a fascinating syncretic nature. In some instances, it is clear that the names of heathen deities have simply been replaced by God, Mary, saints, or angels. In other texts, Christian deities are paralleled with pre-Christian spirits or the awesome powers in nature. Mrs. V. B. was the only healer recorded for this project who included an explicitly

33. St. Nicholas was riding on a white horse
To a white church;
And in the white church,
On a white altar,
Was the Holiest Virgin Mary.

34. O Holiest Mother of God, we ask your help.
Holy Father Anthony, who healed the Lord God's
Great pain, broken bone, seventy joints,
Heal the born and baptized [name]
Of great pain, of the large bone, of the tooth.
A pike is in the sea, my father is in the grave.
From this time forward, in the born and baptized [name]
Teeth shall not hurt. [Spit 3 times]

non-Christian element in her entreaty. Besides the Lord God, Jesus Christ, and the Mother of God, she invoked "seventy-seven and one" sister stars to help her to walk, to work, and to capture the fear of the patient (see Incantations One, Two, and Three, lines 9–10).

Mrs. V. B. invoked the power of the new moon to effect a cure (see Incantation Seven). The moon and other celestial bodies have been common elements in Ukrainian and other Slavic folklore. In a Russian incantation, relief from a sore tooth is sought by enlisting the help of the moon:

Mesiats, ty Mesiats—serebrenye rozhki, zlatyia tvoi nozhki!
Soidi ty, Mesiats, snimi moiu zubnuiu skorb',
Unesi bol' pod oblaka. (Afanas'ev [1865] 1970, 1: 418)[35]

While washing her patient, Mrs. V. B. summoned the water to wash away the fear, sickness, and nerves that had been plaguing the patient. The power of water against evil forces has been well documented in folk medicine. Water is invoked to wash away the evil eye to distant places. A similar Ukrainian incantation also stresses the importance of water in washing away the evil eye:

Pomahaiesh, voda iavlennaia;
Ochyshchaiesh ty, voda iavlennaia.
I luha, i bereha, i seredynu.
Ochyshchai ty, voda iavlennaia,
Moho porozhdennoho ot prozora
Podumana, i pohadana, i vstriechena,[36]

35. Moon, O silver-horned Moon, you have golden feet!
Come out, O Moon, and take away the anguish in my tooth
And carry the pain up to the clouds.

36. You help, O you water before me;
You cleanse, O you water before me,
The meadows, and the banks, and the interior.
Cleanse, O water before me,
My born one from the Evil Eye
Made up, and imagined, and encountered,

I vodianoho i vitrianoho, i zhinots'koho,
I muzhyts'koho, i parubots'koho, i divots'koho.
Pidit' vy, uroky, na soroky,
Na luha, na ochereta,
Na bolota, za moria. (Arandarenko [1849] 1979, 2:231)[37]

Mrs. V. B.'s water incantation referred to water as being "*iordans'ka*" (from the river Jordan). The following incantation calls upon the Jordan's water to cure *neduha*, a general state of sickness:

Vodychko-Iordanychko!
Vmyvaiesh luhy-berehy,
Korinie, bile kaminie,
Umyi seho rshchenoho, chysto vchynenoho
Vid hnivu, nenavysty i vid usiakoho lykha. (Franko 1898, 66)[38]

The fear or sickness itself is treated somewhat as a supernatural power, and it is personified in the incantations. The recorded incantations of the Alberta healers include the appellations *slabist'* (sickness), *strakh* (fear), *zhakh* (horror), *nervy* (nerves), *nenavist'* (hatred), *uroky* (fear sickness), *satana* (satan), *dyiavol* (devil), and *neduha* (illness). They are also often addressed indirectly by epithets such as "from the north," "from the south," "sent upon us," and "sleepy." As they exorcise the evil, the healers often refer to it by the singular pronoun "you."

The following incantations to ward off fear, recorded a century ago

---

37. And of water, and of wind, and of woman,
And of man, and of swain, and of maiden,
Go you, Evil Eye, to the magpies,
To the meadows, to the reeds,
To the bogs, beyond the seas.

38. O water of the Jordan!
You wash the meadows and banks,
Roots, and white rocks,
Wash this baptized, purely created one
Of anger, hatred, and all evil.

in the Poltava region of Ukraine, share the generous use of negative names and adjectives in identifying the problem. Of special note is the relatively frequent use of adjectives referring to animals.

Perepolokh podumanyi, pohadanyi, skotynyi,
Zvirynyi i naslanyi.
Tut tobi ne stoiat', krovy ne ssat',
Zhovtoï kosti ne lamat', a zhyl ne tiahty, a sertsia ne toshnyty.
Pidy sobi na ohni, na dyma, na velyki stepa.
Tam tobi bude pyn'e, huliannie i vsiake masluvannie.
(Miloradovich 1900, 392)[39]

Perepolokh, perepoloshyshche!
Bat'kiv, materyn, cholovichyi,
Zhinochyi, izliakanyi, istrakhnenyi
I kuriachyi, i husiachyi, i
Skots'kyi, i kins'kyi;
I vyklykaiu od tvoïkh ruk,
Od tvoïkh nih, od rusoï kosy,
Od karykh ochei, od biloho tila,[40]

---

39. Fear imagined, guessed, of cattle,
Of wild beasts, and sent forth.
Here you are not to stay, not to suck blood,
Not to break a yellow bone, not to pull at veins, and the heart not to sicken.
Go to the fires, to the smokes, to the vast steppes.
There you will have drink, merriment, and all the good things in life.

40. Fear, o great fear!
Of father, of mother, of man,
Of woman frightened, fearful,
And of chicken, and of goose, and
Of cattle, and of horse;
I call it away from your hands,
From your legs, from your blonde braid,
From your hazel eyes, from white body

Od shchyroho sertsia,
Od narozhenoï, molytvianoï, khreshchenoï Mariï.
(Miloradovich 1900, 68, bk. 3: 392)[41]

Exorcism. Three of the four healers specifically conjured the evil power and then sent it off to some far, unknown place away from the patient. Mrs. V. B. commanded the fear or evil force to go "over mountains and over the sea; where man does not walk; where roosters do not crow; where the wind does not blow; and where the sun does not warm." She exorcised the evil to a place where people do not and could not possibly set foot, commanding it to go to mountains, sands, the sea, and waters. Mrs. J. T. demanded that the evil spirit leave the body for the forest, mountains, and meadows. Mrs. D. M. sent the evil spirit to roots, sands, river banks, forests, and waters.

In commanding the spirits to leave the body for remote and faraway destinations, the healers alluded to additional hindrances designed to make the passage back to the patient more difficult. Mrs. V. B. commanded evil spirits to turn over mountains, sift through sands, and pour through water. As long as the evil force is detained by sifting, pouring, breaking, and turning over natural phenomena, the patient is protected. Such passages are often found in older Slavic and Ukrainian incantations.

The exorcism of evil from specific body parts, the blood, or joints was common to several of the incantations used by the healers. Mrs. V. B.'s first incantation is an excellent example of this: she exorcised evil from the brain, the heart, the viscera, and the spleen. Mrs. D. M. commanded fear to leave the body and blood of her patient.

The incantation below is similar to those of Mrs. V. B. It incorporates a long list of body parts.

41. From your earnest heart,
From the born, blessed, baptized Mary.

Hospody mylostyvyi, pomozhy meni!
Maty Bozha, i stan' meni u pomochi
Sei perepolokh vylyvaty
Iz ïï holovon'ky,
Iz ïï ruchok, iz ïï nizhok,
Iz ïï pal'tsiv, iz ïï sustavtsiv,
Od ïï semydesiat sustav.
Ne ia ieho vylyvaiu, ne ia vyklykaiu,
Sam Hospod' vylyvav i vyklykav
I Matir Bozha v pomochi stoiala,
Si perepolokhy odbirala,
Na Dunai na more zsylala.
Na Dunai na mori simdesiat iazykiv strepechuchys',
Sviatyi misiats' na nebi i Matir Bozha na zemli,
I si perepolokhy zbirala i vitriani,
I khlopiachi i cholovichi
I vykhrovi i blyskovi i hromovi
I koniachi i voliachi i sobachi
I husiachi i kuriachi i hadiuchi[42]

---

42. Merciful Lord, help me!
Mother of God, come to my aid
To pour out this fear
From her head,
From her hands, from her legs,
From her digits, from her joints,
From her seventy joints.
It is not I who am pouring, or conjuring:
The Lord himself has poured out and conjured it,
And the Mother of God stood by to help out,
She removed those fears.
And banished them to the Danube, to the sea.
On the Danube, on the sea, with seventy tongues trembling,
The holy moon in the sky and the Mother of God on Earth,
And she gathered the fear of the winds,
And of boys and of men,
And of whirlwinds, and of lightening bolts, and of thunder,
And of horses, and of oxen, and of dogs,
And of geese, and of chickens, and of snakes,

I zhabiachi i potaini i khlopiachi i zhonochi i divchachi,
I ne ia ïkh vyzyvala,
I ne ia svoïm dukhom podymala,—
Sam Hospod' vyzyvav i svoïm dukhom
Podymav od zhovtoï kosti,
Od chervonoï krovi, od ïï holosu,
Od ïï volosu i od rozhdenoï,
Molytvianoï i khreshchenoï
Raby Bozhoï Mariï. Amin'. (Miloradovich 1900, 68, bk. 3: 393)[43]

The following incantation is used to cure *hostets'* (rheumatism). It is uttered in conjunction with the burning and subsequent extinguishing of nine coals. As in wax ceremony incantations, the formula contains references to body parts and various animals. The incantation is repeated three times. After each repetition, the healer insufflates the patient.

Bozhe pomozhy myni prymovyty,
Use zle zakl'ysty i zamovyty.
Khot' ies bol'ychka, khot' ies skusov,
Khot' ies hostets' sukhyi, khot' hnylyi,
Ie vsi tsi horesty-bolesty,
Koliuchi-boliuchi,[44]

---

43. And of frogs, and of hidden ones, and of boys, and of women, and of girls
And it was not I who conjured them,
And it was not I with my own spirit who blew [away the evil]—
The Lord himself conjured and with his own Spirit
Blew [evil] away from the yellow bone,
From the red blood, from her voice,
From her hair, and from the born,
Blessed, and baptized
Servant of God, Mary. Amen.

44. Lord help me to recite the incantation,
To curse and to conjure all evil.
Though you are a pain, though there you are a whooping cough,
Though you are dry and rotten rheumatism,
You are all of this pain and suffering,
Prickly and sore,

Vizyvaiu, viklykaiu
Z holový, z pid holový,
Z tymiï, z pid tymiï,
Z ochyi, z pid ochyi
Z nosa, z pid nosa,
Z rota, z pid rota,
Z shyï, z pid shyï,
Yz vukh, yz slukh,
Yz potylytsi, z pid potylytsi,
Z plechyi, z pid plechyi,
Z hrudyi, z pid hrudyi,
Z pechinok, z pid pechinok,
Z kyshok, z pid kyshok,
Z simdes'yt' sustavok,
Z kryzhiv, z pid kryzhiv,
Z stehon, z pid stehon,
Yz kolin, z pid kolin,
Yz lytok, z pid lytok,
Yz kotykiv, z pid kotykiv,[45]

---

45. I enjoin and summon you
From the head, from under the head.
From the crown of the head, from under the crown of the head,
From the eyes, from under the eyes,
From the nose, from under the nose,
From the mouth, from under the mouth,
From the neck, from under the neck,
From the ears, from the hearing,
From the nape, from under the nape,
From the shoulders, from under the shoulders,
From the chest, from under the chest,
From the viscera, from under the viscera,
From the guts, from under the guts,
From seventy joints,
From the lower back, from under the lower back,
From the thighs, from under the thighs,
From the knees, from under the knees,
From the calves, from under the calves,
From the ankles, from under the ankles,

Z plesniv, z pid plesniv,
Z pal'tsiv, z pid pal'tsiv,
Z pidoshviv, z pid pidoshviv.
Ia vse zle, vse lykhe vizyvaiu, viklykaiu,
Yz seho khreshchenoho, porozhenoho, molytvennoho [imrek]!
Ydy sobi tam, de psy ne dobrikhuiut,
De kury ne dopivaiut, de liude ne buvaiut,
De sy sluzhby ne pravyï!
Daiu tobi kurku z kur'yty,
Kitku z kot'yty,
Svyniu z poros'yty,
Kachku z kach'yty,
Husku z hus'yty!
Idy sobi, bery sobi, nesy sobi
V syni moria, v hluboki potoky.
Tam ty budesh piskom peresypaty,
V vodi sy kupaty,
V lyst sy zavyvaty!
V hiliu sy kolyshy, [46]

46. From the middle of the feet, from under the middle of the feet,
From the toes, from under the toes,
From the soles, from under the soles.
I enjoin and summon all that is evil, all that is bad,
From this baptized, born, and blessed [name]!
Go there beyond the range of dogs' barking,
Beyond cocks' crowing, where people do not go,
Where church services are not conducted!
I give you a hen with chicks,
A cat with kittens,
A sow with piglets,
A duck with ducklings,
A goose with goslings!
Go away, take [these things] with you, and carry [them] with you
To the blue seas, to deep streams.
There you will sift through sand,
Bathe in water,
Wrap yourself in a leaf!
Swing on a branch,

A seho khreshchenoho, porozhenoho, molytvennoho,
Chystoho v zdoroviu lyshy!
Yyk t'y naishlo rano, rano t'y vidsylaiu,
Yyk t'y naishlo v obidy, v obidy t'y vidsylaiu,
Yyk t'y naishlo v poludny, v poludny t'y vidsylaiu,
Yyk t'y naishlo d'vecheru, v vechir t'y vidsylaiu,
Yyk t'y naishlo v zmerk, u zmerk t'y vidsylaiu,
Yyk t'y naishlo v zavl'yhy, v zavl'yhy t'y vidsylaiu,
Yyk t'y naishlo dos'vita, dos'vita t'y vidsylaiu.
Ia tebe vidsylaiu piit'my pal'ts'ymy,
Shestov dolonev t'y zaklynaiu.
Yyk t'y vid teper zdohoniu,
Zolotymy mechamy tobi holovu zdoimu;
Budu t'y psamy pervakamy trovyty,
Kotamy pervakamy draty,
Sokyramy rubaty, kosamy kosyty, serpamy zh'yty,
Hrabl'ymy rozhribaty, vinykamy rozmitaty!
Tsur z khaty! Pek ty! Skopai sy y strat' sy;
Motsy ne maiesh, krasy ne spyvaiesh,[47]

---

47. And this baptized, born, blessed,
And pure person you will leave in health!
If you were found in the morning, in the morning I send you away.
If you were found at noon, at noon I send you away.
If you were found in the afternoon, in the afternoon I send you away.
If you were found before evening, in the evening I send you away.
If you were found at dusk, at dusk I send you away.
If you were found at bedtime, at bedtime I send you away.
If you were found at dawn, at dawn I send you away.
I send you away with five fingers,
And with the sixth, the palm, I conjure you.
Henceforth when I catch up to you,
I will remove your head with golden swords;
I will send firstborn dogs upon you,
Scratch you with firstborn cats,
With axes I will chop you, with scythes I will cut you, with sickles I will swath you,
With rakes I will rake you, with brooms sweep you away!
Away from the house! Begone! May you be buried and disappear;
You have no power, you will not consume beauty;

Vidkys pryishov, tudy sy nazad obertai!
Ne moim dukhom, ale Bozhym!
Nai Bih dast na vik, tai na lik!
Skachy zdorov! (Shukhevych 1908, 246–7)[48]

Formal Features of the Text

Ia tebe vizyvaiu, ia tebe viklykuiu!
Idy sobi v more!
Tam v pisku sobi hrai, kolachi sobi ïdzh,
Vyno sobi pyi!
Tu ne maiesh sobi dila
Do biloho tila, do rumianoho lytsia,
Zhovtoï kosty skypaty-lupaty,
Span'y vidbyraty, ïdu vidoimaty
I vik korotaty!... (Franko 1898, 69)[49]

The above incantation demonstrates the poetic style and rhythmic structure typical of Slavic incantations. Most of them have recognizable rhythms and rhymes (Sokolov 1956, 244). So, too, do most of the incantations of the wax ceremony healers in Alberta.

One common device is rhythm. The healer may repeat either an entire formula or certain sections of it. This makes memorization of lengthy or

48. Go back whence you came!
Not by my spirit but by God's [power]!
May God grant life and a cure!
Jump up and be healthy!

49. I summon you, I enjoin you!
Go to the sea!
There you may play in the sand, you may eat *kolachi*,
You may drink wine!
Here you have no business
With a white body, a rosy face,
Boiling and ripping a yellow bone,
Taking sleep away, taking nourishment away,
And shortening a lifetime!

complex incantations much easier. Rhythm is often created by reciting similar elements, such as the many body parts discussed above and found in the following brief text.

Pomoshch moia ot Hospoda sotvorshoho nebo i zemliu.
Ïkhav sv. Iurii na voronykh koniakh, na chotyr'okh kolesakh.
Koly rozbihlysia kolesa, rozkotylysia po syn'omu moriu, po chystomu poliu.
Ia izhoniaiu bil'mo ot khreshchenoho raba Bozhoho [imrek]
Vyhovoriuiu v kostei, v moshchei,
V tisnykh plechei, v synikh pechenei,
Iz buinoï holovy, v chutkykh ushei,
Iz shchyroho zhyvota iz [...?] sertsa,
Z horychoï krovy, z zhovtykh kostei,
Z solodkoho mochu.
U raba Bozhoho [imrek] sl'oza iz oka i bil'mo ot oka!
(Efimenko 1874, 9)[50]

Recurring repetitions are sometimes intoned in multiples of the magical number three. The numbers three and nine figured prominently among the healers interviewed for this study. Mrs. V. B. and Mrs. D. M. recited their lengthy incantations three times per session. The incantations they used for each of the three pourings were quite similar.

These numbers were also reflected in the ritual actions that took place during the ceremony. Mrs. V. B. and Mrs. D. M. both poured wax three

50. My help comes from the Lord, who created Heaven and Earth.
St. George was riding on four black horses on four wheels
When the wheels came off, [and] rolled over the blue sea and over the open field.
I drive out the cataract from the baptized servant of God [name].
I conjure in the bones, in the body,
In the tight shoulders, in the blue viscera,
From the strong head, in the sensitive ears,
From the very stomach[?], from the [... ?] heart,
From the hot blood, from the yellow bones,
And from the sweet urine.
In the servant of God [name] a tear from the eye and the cataract from the eye!

times—once above the head of the patient, once at the chest area, and once behind the patient or at the patient's back. Mrs. K. W. poured wax three times above each of three different body locations, for a total of nine pourings. Mrs. M. H. poured water into her bowl in three distinct motions. Mrs. V. B.'s patients sipped water three times from a shot glass.

In the minds of healers and their patients today, the numbers three and seven have taken on a Christian significance. The number three is representative of the Father, the Son, and the Holy Spirit, and seven is the day on which God rested after creating the world. According to Boltarovych (1980, 112), these numbers were considered holy and were referred to as "*znaky, danymy Bohom*" (signs given by God).

Thompson explains the significance of these numbers in other cultures. The number nine was equated with wisdom, power, mystery, and protection. "Three ... was regarded as a Holy number and has always been looked upon with favor in all things. It was the number of the Trinity, signifying plenty and fruitfulness, and the third day was venerated as being one of good fortune" (1946, 162–4). The number three represented wholeness or perfection in the primitive concept of the trinity of body, soul, and spirit. Thompson argues that the number seven was regarded as even more mystical than the number three because it bonded two sets of threes together. The number seven had divine significance for magicians and healers. The Pythagoreans associated it with the seven days of the week, the seven planets, seven known metals, and the seven ages of man.

Numbers figured prominently in Mrs. D. M.'s second incantation. Her formula contained a set of running numbers that began with the number nine and ended at zero. The following cure for sore eyes, recorded in Cornwall, England, contains the same run of numbers. Nine burning coals are cast into a bowl of water when the following formula is recited. Similar formulas can be found in other non-Slavic incantations.

Underneath this hazelin mote,
There's a braggoty worm with a speckled throat,
Nine double is he;
Now from nine double to eight double,

And from eight double to seven double,
And from seven double to six double,
And from six double to five double,
And from five double to four double,
And from four double to three double,
And from three double to two double,
And from two double to one double,
And from one double to no double,
No double hath he! (Black 1970, 122–23)

Colours also have a symbolic significance in healing. The colours red, yellow, and white were used frequently in incantations by Mrs. V. B.: "*Chervonu krov ne pyi, bile kilo ne sushy, zhovtu kist' ne lupai*" (Do not drink red blood, dehydrate a white body, [or] strip a yellow bone). Mrs. D. M. drew attention to a white body in her first incantation, which she intoned over the head of the patient. Two healers insisted that their best wax pourings were achieved when they used black cast-iron frying pans to melt the wax.

Red is considered one of the most powerful colours. Evil spirits and the diseases they wreak find the colour most obnoxious. In some parts of Britain, patients are asked to rest on red bedsheets or wear small pieces of red cloth on their bodies in order to get well. White is considered to be the opposite of red: it is cold, pure, and flawless. Yellow does not appear to be an important colour in the healing rituals of other cultures, but in Ukrainian culture it is often associated with bones and appears frequently in traditional Ukrainian healing incantations.

The Contemporary Context

In the wax ceremony explicitly Christian elements are combined with others whose pre-Christian origins are evident. This syncretism is marked, both in the ritual and in the incantations.

Syncretism in the Ritual

With the exception of "praying" and making the sign of the cross over the patient, water, or wax, few other actions in the wax ceremony would normally be considered part of official Christianity. Acts such as insufflation or washing the patient are pre-Christian in origin. They were eventually incorporated into church usage, and their purposes were redefined. Beeswax can be called "Christian" since it is prescribed for church candles and since "bees are wise and talk to God." This "Christian-ness" is only partial, however, as the use of beeswax in the wax ceremony is clearly outside official church practice. The same is true of the use of Gospel ribbons and altar cloths, for example. They are clearly associated with the church and with the power of its prayer. But they are used in a way that suggests a non-Christian (likely pre-Christian) sensibility for magic.

The incorporation of pre-Christian elements in Christian tradition makes it difficult to classify elements in either category. The categorizations in Table 4, therefore, are only suggestive, based on the general perceptions of Christianity in the Ukrainian community of western Canada. Selected elements are listed in the first column if they are recognized as explicitly Christian. The second column includes elements found in the informants' Christian traditions, but appearing in the wax ceremony with significant changes. The third column lists elements that are more clearly beyond regular Christian practice.

Table 4. Syncretic Elements in the Wax Ceremony

Explicitly Christian	Quasi-Christian	Non-Christian
Crossing oneself before beginning	Insufflation	Tools such as knives, rocks, and combs
Praying for intercession from God, the Virgin Mary, or the saints	Washing	Addition of salt or garlic to healing water
No healing on Sundays or church holidays	Holy water	Specific healing days or times
	Easter candles	Associating special times of the day with magical powers
	Holy or church cloths	Reading/interpreting wax shapes
	Fumigating (incensing)	Conjuring
	Facing east	Wearing protective amulets
	Beeswax (bees talk to God)	
	Disposing of healing water where no person will tread	
	Reference to the number three or multiples of three	
	Importance and power associated with colours	
	Donations or payment for the healer's services redirected to the local church	
	Making wishes for health and happiness	

Syncretism in the Incantations

Syncretism is particularly clear in the formulas uttered by the healers. The classification of Christian and non-Christian elements in Table 5 takes into account only the incantations used by informants interviewed for this study. Again, the categories are not discrete.

The status of the wax ceremony as an activity somewhat on the margins between Christian teaching and non-Christian practice seems to perplex neither the healer nor the patient. Both believe that the healer is merely an intercessor between the patient and God, who ultimately grants a cure and the subsequent restoration to health.

On the other hand, the official church's view is quite different. It has repeatedly condemned these healers and their craft.

Table 5. Syncretic Elements in the Incantations

Healer	Explicitly Christian	Quasi-Christian or Non-Christian
V. B.	Refers to the Lord God, Jesus Christ, and the Virgin Mary	Exorcism of fear from body parts and joints
	Calls water "Jordan Water"	Prayers to seventy-seven and one stars
		Expulsion of sickness and evil to far-away places where no human will go
		References to water, fire, and garlic
		Praying to the moon
		Reference to evil spirits
S. K.	Recites the Lord's Prayer	Use of numbers (9–0) to exorcise evil
D. M.	Invokes the Father, Son, and Holy Spirit three times	Expulsion of evil to places where no human will tread
	Refers to the Lord God, Jesus Christ, the Mother of God, and St. Nicholas	
J. T.	Refers to the Virgin Mary, the Lord God, and all saints who have power	Expulsion of evil to places where no human will tread

Canadian Adaptations

The wax ceremony has been very well preserved and is practiced today in much the same fashion as it has been for many generations. While the ceremony remains steeped in tradition and authentic in form, it has undergone some adaptations. Some changes have been introduced to suit conditions as they have evolved in Alberta. Other changes seem to have emerged because each successive generation reinterprets the importance and meaning of the ceremony. The changes are tabulated in Table 6. The malleability of the ceremony has contributed to its endurance and survival.

Traditionally, the water used in the wax ceremony was drawn from a natural "living" source *(zhyve dzherelo)* such as a well, stream, or river. While Ukrainian Canadians lived in rural communities or on farms, they had easier access to well or running water. In the early years of pioneer life in Canada, healers normally used well water. As they developed their homesteads or moved to urban areas, running water replaced hand-drawn well water. All of the healers interviewed for this study admitted that the water for the wax ceremony should come from a well. However, they all rationalized that the water they got from their taps was as effective as well water for curing.

Well water is desirable for practical reasons. When water is drawn from a well, it is very cold. Several healers said that well water was ice-cold and therefore molten wax congealed much more quickly in it. Mrs. V. B. sometimes chose to add ice cubes to her water in order to chill it to the coldest temperature possible.

Water for the wax ceremony was traditionally drawn before sunrise. Of the seven healers interviewed, Mrs. K. W. was the only one who made a point of drawing water from the tap before the sun came up. She believed this water had the greatest curative powers. While several of the other healers had heard of the importance of drawing water before sunrise, none of them practiced this aspect of the ritual.

Most of the healers had heard about days that were specifically reserved for men or women. Several of them took these days into account when making arrangements with patients. Mrs. V. B. and Mr. P. G., however, were in such demand that they came to ignore the concept of special days so that they could comply with all the requests they received for their services. In Ukraine it was not uncommon for every village to have at least one healer who was versed in the wax ceremony. In Alberta, however, healers have been in short supply, while the demand for their services has remained high. As a result, the concept of designated healing days has sometimes been ignored so that healers can treat as many patients as possible.

Most of the healers interviewed for this study claimed that it was more effective to perform the wax ceremony in the morning, before noon. Again, in order to make themselves as accessible as possible, all of the healers except Mrs. J. T. performed their healing throughout the day. In emergencies Mrs. V. B. was known to pour wax even at night.

Congealed wax shapes have traditionally been interpreted or read. While some of the healers continued to include the reading as part of their ceremony, several claimed to be unable to understand the various shapes. When patients and healers were asked how important the interpretation of the congealed wax shapes was, most said that it was not an essential part of the ceremony. The only exception was Mrs. V. B., who placed much emphasis on interpreting the hardened wax shapes. Clearly, patient and healer alike felt that the energy—the entire experience—of the wax ceremony provided the cure, and not any one part of it.

Beeswax was plentiful in Ukraine. Most villages would have had their own beekeepers, and beeswax was readily available for wax pouring. While beeswax is available in Alberta, it is less common than paraffin wax, especially in urban centres. While the healers preferred to use beeswax, they sometimes mixed in paraffin wax.

In Ukraine food was often used as payment for healing services. In the early years of Ukrainian settlement in Alberta, money was not a readily available commodity. Patients often opted to pay for healers' services with food from their farms: eggs, cream, or chickens were common examples of acceptable offerings. Money, however, could also be given. Several healers said they could remember that the acceptable amount was from five to twenty cents. While today's healers still receive gifts, money has become the most common form of payment.

Table 6. Canadian Adaptations of the Wax Ceremony

Component	Earlier Tradition	Adaptation
Water	Drawn from a well	Poured from a tap or natural source
Water temperature	Naturally cold	Add ice cubes
Time of water drawing	Before sunrise	At time of healing
Specific days	Men's and women's days	Any day but Sunday
Wax pouring time	Before noon	Any time
Wax shapes interpreted	Always	Sometimes
Wax type	Beeswax	Beeswax and some times paraffin
Payment	Foodstuffs, goods, money	Money, occasional gifts

Patient Profile

Table 7 lists the sex, approximate age, and profession of each patient. Though most of the patients treated by the wax ceremony are children, adults seek healing as well. Adults were selected as informants for this study. Of the twenty-four informants who had sought the services of a lay healer more than once, nine were men. The informants ranged in age from twenty-five to seventy and had varied backgrounds. Some were students, some were farmers or housewives, and others were well-paid professionals. There appears to be no correlation between professional background, age or, sex and belief in the wax ceremony.

All of the patients firmly believed in the powers that their respective healers claimed to possess. They were convinced that the healers were working by the will of God and that their source of power was good, not evil. When queried as to their religious convictions, patients all said that they believed in God. Many attended church.

The patients seemed to believe that simply sharing their bad experiences with the healer while having the wax ceremony performed was enough to alleviate their symptoms. They said that the ceremony forced them to dig up bad things that had happened in the past and to bring them to the fore, where they could be dealt with.

Table 7. Patient Profile

Patient	Sex	Approx. Age	Occupation
T. D.	M	30	Ph.D. student
L. N.	M	30	White-collar
O. S.	F	45	Blue-collar
H. K.	F	55	Housewife
R. B.	M	40	White-collar
E. B.	M	45	White-collar
B. B.	M	70	Retired
D. B.	M	50	White-collar
S. B.	F	45	Housewife
M. B.	F	30	White-collar
V. J.	F	35	Housewife
V. M.	M	25	M.A. student
S. W.	F	40	Housewife
A. Y.	F	60	Housewife
Vi. B.	F	35	Housewife
S. N.	F	55	Housewife
Anon.	F	55	White-collar
H. S.	M	35	Artist
H. B.	F	70	Housewife
O. H.	F	50	White-collar
N. D.	F	50	Housewife
M. K.	F	60	Housewife
J. B.	M	70	Retired

Mrs. V. B.'s family was especially supportive of her healing practice. She and her powers were revered by many family members. The many patients who used her services as a healer attest to her popularity and to the large number of people who believe in the wax ceremony. The six other healers all said they had many requests from the public to pour wax, and that if they wanted to they could be busy pouring every day.

Mrs. V. B. said that her patients included many Romanians. Mrs. J. T. said that she often poured wax for Italians, who believed in the ceremony as much as her Ukrainian patients. All of the healers claimed to have patients who were "English," that is, not belonging to any ethnic group.

The following brief descriptions of selected informants and their attitudes toward the wax ceremony shed some light on the range of its significance to people in Alberta.

Mrs. H. B. is a housewife in her seventies. She knows about all sorts of other cures and remedies besides the wax ceremony. She has been to a wax healer several times in her life and firmly believes in the ceremony. While she has never practised wax healing, she gave special tea mixtures to her son when he was in hospital. She has treated her relatives' fear sickness by fumigating them as she burned some of the material that was believed to have caused the fear. Mrs. H. B. very much believes in God, but at the same time she is very superstitious.

Mrs. M. K. is a daughter of Mrs. V. B. She is a housewife in her sixties. She is known as the person in the family who is able to tell fortunes using cards. She says she learned to do the card readings from her mother. Like her siblings, Mrs. M. K. is very religious. She also knows of many superstitions and, like Mrs. N. D., says that for the most part, only old people believe in the power of these superstitions, or "*bobony*" as she calls to them.

Mrs. O. H. is a professional woman in her fifties. While she has never undergone the wax ceremony, her mother took her brother to a wax healer when he was a young boy. Mrs. O. H. says that her brother's epilepsy cleared up after he was treated. She remains a firm believer in the power of the ceremony.

Mr. E. B. is a professional about forty-five years of age. He has been to his grandmother, Mrs. V. B., several times. He has also taken his children to her to have the wax ceremony performed. He has a recording of his grandmother's incantation and has performed the ceremony for his own children. While playing Mrs. V. B.'s incantation on tape, Mr. E. B. performs the associated rituals. He believes that some day he will take the ceremony over and become the family practitioner. He also hopes that his son will take over the healing from him some day. Mr. E. B. stated that the relief that is experienced by patients who have had the wax ceremony performed for them comes from their minds actively digging up bad things that have happened in the past and bringing them to the fore. In so doing, the patient deals with his or her problems. He says that once a bad experience has been shared, it is no longer a bad experience. Mr. E. B. is keenly interested in the wax ceremony and is a strong proponent of it.

Mrs. O. S. is a blue-collar worker in her late forties. She has never had the wax ceremony performed, but she has accompanied her mother on several visits to Mrs. V. B. While she recognizes the power the ceremony and the healer have, she refuses to believe in it because she does not know the source of the power. She said she was afraid of it.

Mrs. V. J. is a housewife approximately thirty five years of age. She seems to have spent a great deal of time with Mrs. V.B., her grandmother, learning about her healing. She knows of special rituals that her grandmother performed that none of the other informants mentioned. She has the wax ceremony performed by Mrs. V. B. frequently. She said that when her grandmother placed her hands on her head before blowing away the spirits, she felt like something had been lifted off of her. Mrs. V. J. is somewhat interested in taking over the ceremony, but feels that her husband and young family command most of her attention.

Mrs. Vi. B. is a housewife in her late thirties. Mrs. V. B. is her grandmother. Both Mrs. Vi. B. and her children have had the wax ceremony performed by the grandmother. She believes in her grandmother's powers and the positive effects that are wrought by the ceremony. So intrigued were they by the process, that she and her brother melted some beeswax and poured it into cold water to see what shapes they could discern. After repeated pourings, Mrs. Vi. B. said that neither she nor her brother were able to get anything other than a smooth surface on the wax. She believes that only someone with the power to cure like her grandmother could pour wax and have figures take shape in the wax. Mrs. Vi. B. said that people feel good after her grandmother crosses them and gives them the blessed water to drink. She said that the family is kept together by Mrs. V. B. spending time with individual members. Her grandmother is the family therapist, the psychologist who will talk to you. She said that she feels her grandmother probably knew everything there was to know about a person and, as such, provided good counselling.

Mr. L. N. is a white-collar worker in his thirties. He is another grandson of Mrs. V. B. While Mr. L. N. believes in the wax ceremony, he seemed more reluctant to openly endorse it than some of his siblings. When asked if he believed in the ceremony and in his grandmother's healing abilities, he said he is not superstitious, but was not willing to take chances. Mr. L. N. felt that the important part of the ceremony was to bring the fear that plagues one to the fore in the mind. He referred to the wax ceremony as a mental healing and, like his cousin Mrs. V. J., felt that when he left his grandmother's home he was leaving something behind.

Mr. T. D. is another of Mrs. V. B.'s grandsons. He is a student in his twenties. He believes his grandmother possesses magical and mystical qualities. He has had her pour wax for him several times. He claims to have been cured of stuttering by Mrs. V. B. He is a strong believer in the wax ceremony and said that his grandmother's curing is psychological, not physiological. The patient, he says, cures himself. Mr. T. D. was the person for whom Mrs. V. B. had most recently poured wax. While he felt that she was now less accurate with her incantations and ritual because of her age and failing memory, he said she had diagnosed several of his problems. After the pouring he said he felt much more at ease.

Mr. V. M. is a student in his mid-twenties. He was taken to a wax pourer twice by his mother when they still lived in Ukraine. Mr. V. M. seemed a bit skeptical about the healers and their ability to cure. However, he does believe that his severe nightmares and sleepwalking in his youth ceased as a result of the wax ceremony. Mr. V. M. said that he believed his mother when she said that women healers who have the true gift of healing do not live long lives.

The Survival of the Wax Ceremony

In Ukrainian villages, the wax ceremony had long been a meaningful method of reducing stress. The healer who performed this ceremony was able to restore harmony and equilibrium: by healing patients, she or he helped to reintegrate them into society. After migrating to Canada, the practitioners of the wax ceremony continued functioning in a minority subculture within Canadian society. As Ukrainian immigrants to Canada settled into their new lives and developed and expanded economically, they became less dependent upon their group for moral and financial sustenance. The Ukrainian bloc settlements slowly began eroding as families made their way to rural communities or urban centres. Soon came the "English" doctor—the representative of professional medicine. In spite of an apparently hostile environment in the New World, the wax ceremony remains in great demand more than one hundred years after Ukrainian immigration to Canada began.

Modern medicine became widespread in eastern European villages only late in the ninteenth century. Given their conservative tendencies, the peasants sometimes had reservations about it. Fear sickness or restlessness could be easily diagnosed and cured by the wax healer who shared common etiological assumptions with the patient. This, however, was not true of mainstream practitioners. Min'ko writes of Belarusians who refused to follow their doctor's orders. They believed that the doctor was powerless because he was not working with God: "*Koly Boh ne pomozhet, to i doktor ne pomozhet*" (If God does not help, then the doctor cannot help; Min'ko 1969, 50). Domanyts'kyi writes that Volhynian villagers sought the help of professional medical practitioners only after going to their local healers. The villagers considered the medical profession "*pans'ka vyhadka*"—an invention of the rich (Domanyts'kyi 1905, 101).

Headaches, stomachaches, toothaches, infections, and other health problems could be alleviated by mainstream medical doctors. However, modern medicine could not always compete with the wax ceremony. No medical textbook could prescribe how to deal with powerful spirits causing psychological and physical illness. The ceremony continued to flourish in Alberta because of the demand that only lay healers could fill. Even today Ukrainians continue to visit the wax healer.

Several informants said that if God did not help to cure a person of his fear, no doctor could help: "no matter how good or how much specialization a doctor has, when it comes to wax, he is unable to do it. Like now, they give you pills for your nerves, but it's not the same. But it will never be as effective as will that [wax ceremony]; as when she [Mrs. V. B.] pours the wax, she believes in the prayer. She says the cure is not from her but from God" (Mr. J. B. [Interview 29, 192]).

Mr. J. B. said that professional doctors of Ukrainian descent sometimes sent their patients to a *baba*, or wax healer. He remembered Dr. Y. who worked in Shandro, Alberta. According to Mr. J. B., this doctor sent many of his patients to wax pourers for relief (Interview 29, 190).

The wax ceremony is performed in the comfort of the healer's home. In rare instances, some healers, like Mrs. M. H. or Mrs. V. B., make house calls if the patient is unable to travel to the healer. In these cases, too, the healing takes place in a home environment rather than in a medical institution. All of the healers in this study had a "touch of Ukraine" in their homes. Mr. P. G. had many icons. Mrs. D. M. had embroidered cloths and carved items associated with Ukrainian culture. When compared to a doctor's more formal, often sterile office surroundings, it becomes clear which setting would help to make the patient feel more relaxed and comfortable. The patient can visually relate to the wax healer via shared cultural symbols. According to Russell, the home "provides ... a feeling of security.... It is a setting which is supportive of the ... [healer's] authority" (1981, 12).

On average, a patient can expect to spend upwards of one hour with the wax healer. All of the healers begin by speaking to the patient not only about the illness, but also about general things, such as family, mutual friends, or the weather. The healer expresses an interest in the personal life of the patient. Such conversation relaxes the patient and eases the purging of emotions. The patient opens up to the healer over tea or lunch, which the healer usually prepares specially for the patient: friendship, trust, and a bond develop.

The wax healer's treatment of the patient is in sharp contrast to the professional world, where doctors rarely know their patients' names and appointments are often scheduled at fifteen-minute intervals. In such an environment there is little room for sharing and understanding. Even critics of folk medicine acknowledge lay healers' approachability and warmth. Cobb, who refers to folk healers as "quacks," writes that patients visit them in search of reassurance, hope, recovery, kindness, consideration, and communication (1954, 69).

There is no doubt that healers who practice the wax ceremony enjoy a very privileged status within the Ukrainian community. They are held in high regard by their patients. Their knowledge of healing is acquired through special channels, and their skills are innate. Theirs is a privileged and mysterious calling. They and their secrets will continue to exist as part of the social fabric of Ukrainian culture.

The Power of Folk Medicine

Frank lists four criteria for effective folk curing: (1) the faith of the healers in their own abilities to cure; (2) the faith of the patient in the healer's abilities; (3) acknowledgement of the disease by the social group; and (4) acceptance of the healing method by the group (1959, 21). According to these criteria, the wax ceremony can be considered effective folk medicine.

All of the patients interviewed for this study claimed that the wax ceremony had worked for them. It had relieved them of their psychological and physical ailments. They were satisfied with the healers and the cures they had wrought. Equally, healers felt that they were very successful in their own work. If a patient did not recover after one pouring, the healer relinquished responsibility by explaining that the fear had been left unattended by the patient too long.

Perhaps the magical and mystical aspects of the wax ceremony have served to preserve it. In the minds of both patient and healer, the ceremony is a very special and powerful phenomenon. The rewards that wax healers enjoy are numerous. They are made to feel important in their families, local communities, and beyond. Their often extroverted nature, coupled with their genuine desire and need to help people, brings them friendship, fame, and, in some instances, fortune. They are needed by the community as healers, psychologists, and confidants. From generation to generation these healers have passed on a legacy, culture, and tradition.

In more than one hundred years of existence in Canada, the wax ceremony has remained true to form and popular as ever. The healers who practice it propagate a sense of community and social interdependence. Their importance goes far beyond the realm of healing. They continue to have a significant place in the cultural continuum.

Predictions for the Future

It is my guess that the demand for the wax ceremony will remain high for another generation. However, this genre of Ukrainian folk medicine, like other indigenous practices brought from Ukraine, could eventually die out. Language loss, assimilation, science, and technology have taken their toll. It does not appear that fourth- and fifth-generation Ukrainian Canadians are playing an active role in preserving the ceremony. At best, their interest can be described as curiosity or an attempt to "get in touch" with their culture and roots.

Resilient thus far, the wax ceremony will continue to adapt along with changing worldviews as long as successive generations consider it to be culturally relevant. If patients continue to value the wax healers and share disease etiologies with them, the ceremony will survive. Like beeswax over a flame, it will melt, reshape, and be interpreted anew.

Glossary

Baba. Old woman; healer.
Babka. Old woman (diminutive); healer.
Babs'kyi den'. Women's day; a day when women may be healed.
Babtsia. Old woman (diminutive); healer.
Babunia. Old woman (diminutive); healer.
Baba-povytukha. Old woman, midwife; healer.
Baila. Murmurer; healer.
Bobony. Superstitions.
Braty hroshi. To take money (for a healing session).
Chaklunka. Conjurer; healer.
Charivnytsia. Conjurer; healer.
Charnytsia. Conjurer; healer.
Chudesnytsia. Wonder-worker; healer.
Chytaty visk. To interpret wax shapes.
Do sebe. (To pour wax) towards oneself.
Hlukhyi koner. Corner behind a door.
Khlops'kyi den'. Men's day; a day when men may be healed.
Khoroba. Sickness.
Koldunytsia. Sorceress; healer.
Kydalo ioho. He had convulsions (i.e., epilepsy).
Lehshe meni. I feel better.
Liak. Fear.
Lyshylo mene. It has left me; I feel better.
Mishanyi den'. Mixed day; a day when men and women may be healed.
Molytva. Incantation; prayer.
Na viglie. Counterclockwise.
Nahalas. Incantation.
Naliakatysia. To become afraid.
Nastrashytysia. To become afraid.
Obavnytsia. Conjurer; healer.
Pade na dity. (A curse or fright) befalls children.
Peredaty. To pass on (one's healing knowledge).
Pereishlo mene. It has left me; I feel better.

Pereliak. Fear.
Perepolokh. Fear.
Perepudytysia. To become afraid.
Perestrakh. Fear.
Pidibraty kohos'. To choose someone (to pass on one's healing knowledge to).
Pidkurennia. Fumigation.
Pidkuriuvalo. Fumigation "bundle."
Pity na visk. To go to have wax poured.
Porozhnyi den'. Empty day; one or two days before a new moon when wax is not to be poured.
Potvornytsia. Seeress; healer.
Proklinnytsia. Witch; healer.
Prymivka. Incantation.
Prymivnytsia. Sorceress; healer.
Prymovliaty. To utter an incantation.
Rozumitysia na visk. To (be able to) interpret wax shapes.
Shcho visk skazhe. The shapes shown ("told") by the wax.
Sheptukha. Murmurer; healer.
Skazaty paru sliv vid sebe. To utter an incantation.
Slabist'. Sickness.
Slabist' pereimaiese. To catch an illness.
Slova. Incantation.
Starukha. Old woman; healer.
Starushka. Old woman (diminutive); healer.
Strakh. Fear.
Sviachenne. Fumigation "bundle."
Vaks. Wax.
Vid sebe. (To pour wax) away from oneself.
Vid sebe znaty. To know an incantation by heart.
Vidkachuvaty strakh. To draw out fear with an egg.
Vid'ma. Witch; healer.
Vidmal'ovatysia. To make wax shapes.
Vidshipchennia. Incantation.
Vidunka. Wise woman; witch; healer.
Viliaie se. To make wax shapes.

Vishchunytsia. Wise woman; healer.
Visk. Wax.
Visk perelovyt'sia. The wax will harden.
Visk vylyvaty. To pour wax.
Visk zlyvaty. To pour wax.
Vorozhka. Fortuneteller; witch; healer.
Vorozhbytka. Fortuneteller; witch; healer.
Vorozhylia. Fortuneteller; witch; healer.
Vydunytsia. Wise woman; healer.
Zabobony. Superstitions.
Zachytuvannia. Incantation.
Zadavnenyi strakh. Fear that has been left untreated.
Zahovor. Incantation.
Zaklynannia. Incantation.
Zamovlennia. Incantation.
Zamovliannia. Incantation.
Zaspanyi strakh. Fear that has been left untreated overnight while the afflicted slept.
Zhena-vorozhylia. Witch; healer.
Zhinochyi den'. Women's day; a day when women may be healed.
Znakha. Wise woman; healer.
Znakharka. Wise woman; healer.
Zolotarykha. Golden conjurer; healer.

List of Interviews[51]

Interview 1. Recorded interview with T. D. and V. J., October 1986.
Interview 2. Recorded with L. N., October 1986.
Interview 3. Recorded with O. S., November 1986.
Interview 4. Recorded with H. K., October 1986.
Interview 5. Recorded with V. B., September 1986.
Interview 6. Recorded with V. B. by Kathy Starchuk-Horobec, 1971.
Interview 7. Recorded with R. B., October 1986.
Interview 8. Recorded with E. B., October 1986.
Interview 9. Recorded with S. K., October 1986.
Interview 10. Recorded with B. B., October 1986.
Interview 11. Unrecorded discussion with J. T., 1986.
Interview 12. Unrecorded discussion with J. T., 1986.
Interview 13. Unrecorded discussion with M. H., 1986.
Interview 14. Unrecorded discussion with P. G., 1986.
Interview 15. Recorded with K. W., September 1986.
Interview 16. Recorded with D. B., S. B., and M. B., October 1986.
Interview 17. Recorded with V. J., October 1986.
Interview 18. Recorded with V. M., October 1986.
Interview 19. Recorded with S. W., October 1986.
Interview 20. Recorded with A. Y., November 1986.
Interview 21. Recorded with Vi. B., October 1986.
Interview 22. Recorded with S. N., October 1986.
Interview 23. Recorded with Anon., August 1986.
Interview 24. Recorded with H. S., September 1986.
Interview 25. Recorded with H. B., September 1986.
Interview 26. Recorded with O. H., September 1986.
Interview 27. Recorded with D. M., April 1987.
Interview 28. Recorded with N. D. and M. K., October 1986.
Interview 29. Recorded with J. B., October 1986.
Recorded video session with S. B., 1984.
Recorded video session with V. B., October 1986.

51. All interviews, except no. 6, were conducted by Rena Hanchuk.

Bibliography

Abbott, G. F. 1903. *Macedonian Folklore*. Cambridge: Cambridge University Press.

Ackernecht, Erwin. 1942. "Problems of Primitive Medicine." *Bulletin of the History of Medicine* 2: 503–21.

Afanas'ev, A. [1865–69] 1970. *Poeticheskiia vozzreniia slavian na prirodu* (The poetic outlook of Slavs on nature), 3 vols. Reprint, The Hague: Mouton.

Alexander, Alex E. 1975. *Russian Folklore: An Anthology in English Translation*. Belmont, Mass.: Nordland.

Apple, Dorrian. 1960. "How Laymen Define Illness." *Journal of Health and Human Behavior* 1: 219–25.

Arandarenko, Nikolai. [1849] 1979. "Zapiski o Poltavskoi gubernii" (Notes on Poltava province). *Gubernskiia pravleniia* (Poltava) Reprint, 3 vols., Ann Arbor: University Microfilms International.

Black, William George. 1970. *Folk-Medicine: A Chapter in the History of Culture*. New York: Burt Franklin.

Blum, Richard and Eva Blum. 1965. *Health and Healing in Rural Greece: A Study of Three Communities*. Stanford: Stanford University Press.

Bogatyrev, Pierre. 1929. *Actes magiques, rites et croyances en Russie Subcarpathique* (Magic acts, rituals, and beliefs in Subcarpathian Rus'). Paris: Honoré Champion.

Bogdanovich, A. V. 1877. *Sbornik svedenii o Poltavskoi gubernii* (Collection of information on Poltava province). Poltava: Tipografiia Gubernskago pravleniia.

Boltarovych, Z. Ie. 1980. *Narodne likuvannia ukraïntsiv Karpat kintsia XIX–pochatku XX stolittia* (Folk medicine of the Ukrainians of the Carpathians at the end of the nineteenth–beginning of the twentieth century). Kyiv: Naukova dumka.

———. 1983. "Narodna medytsyna ta veterynariia" (Folk medicine and veterinary medicine). In *Boikivshchyna: Istoryko-etnohrafichne doslidzhennia* (The Boiko region: A historico-ethnographic study), edited by Iu. Hoshko, 226–32. Kyiv: Naukova dumka.

———. 1987. "Narodna medytsyna ta veterynariia" (Folk medicine and veterinary medicine). In *Hutsulshchyna: Istoryko-etnohrafichne doslidzhennia* (The Hutsul region: A historico-ethnographic study), edited by Iu. Hoshko, 272–86. Kyiv: Naukova dumka.

Borovsky, M. 1984. "Beekeeping." In *Encyclopedia of Ukraine*, vol 1, edited by Volodymyr Kubijovyč, 190–1. Toronto: University of Toronto Press.

Borovykovs'kyi, Levko. [1829] 1971. "Marusia." In his *Tvory* (Works), 21–7. Kyiv: Molod.

Brailovskii, S. 1891. "Sposob lecheniia ot sglaza" (The method of treating the evil eye). *Zhivaia starina*, no. 3: 224.

Bromlei, Iu. V. 1976. "Narodnaia meditsina kak predmet etnograficheskikh issledovanii" (Folk medicine as a subject of ethnographic studies). *Sovetskaia etnografiia*, no. 5: 3–18.

Camp, John. 1978. *The Healer's Art: The Doctor through History.* London: Frederick Muller.

"Chary v suchasnii medytsyni" (Incantations in contemporary medicine). 1961. In *Kalendar-al'manakh "Novoho shliakhu,"* 127–30.

Chomik, Lori-Lee. 1982. "Folklore Medicine." Student essay for UKR 326. University of Alberta.

Chubinskii, P. P. 1872. *Trudy etnografichesko-statisticheskoi ekspeditsii v Zapadno-Russkii krai* (Works of the ethnographic-statistical expedition to the West Russian Land). Vol. 1. St. Petersburg: Imperatorskoe russkoe geograficheskoe obshchestvo.

Cobb, B. 1954. "Why Do People Detour to Quacks?" *The Psychiatric Bulletin*, no. 3: 66–9.

Crépeau, Pierre, ed. 1985. *Médicine et religion populaires/Folk Medicine and Religion.* Ottawa: National Museum of Man.

Dąbrowska, Stanisława. 1902. "Poszukiwania" (The quest). *Wisła*, no. 16: 425–9.

Dmitriukov, A. 1831. "Nravy, obychai i obraz zhizhni v Sudzhenskom uezde, Kurskoi gubernii" (Customs, rituals, and the way of life in Sudzha county, Kursk province). *Moskovskii telegraf*, no. 10–11: 359–77.

Domanyts'kyi, Vasyl'. 1905. "Narodna medytsyna v Rovens'komu poviti na Volyni" (Folk medicine in Rivne county in Volhynia). In

Materyialy do ukraïns'ko-rus'koï etnol'ogiï 6: 100.

Dömötör, Tekla. 1982. *Hungarian Folk Beliefs*. Budapest: Athenaeum Printing House.

Dorson, Richard M. 1964. *Buying the Wind: Regional Folklore in the United States*. Chicago: University of Chicago Press.

Dragomanov, Mikhail P. 1876. *Malorusskiia narodnyia predaniia i razskazy* (Little Russian [Ukrainian] folk tradition and tales). Kyiv: Russkoe geograficheskoe obshchestvo.

Drazheva, Raina. 1973. "Obriady sviazannye s okhranoi zdorov'ia v prazdnike letnego solntsestoianiia u vostochnikh i iuzhnikh slavian" (Rituals connected with the preservation of health in the summer solstice celebrations of the East and South Slavs). *Sovetskaia etnografiia*, no. 6: 109–19.

Dumka, Mykyta. 1968. "Medytsyna karpats'kykh ukraïntsiv" (Medicine of the Carpathian Ukrainians). *Narodna tvorchist' ta etnohrafiia*, no. 5: 45–6.

Dundes, Alan. 1980. *Interpreting Folklore*. Bloomington: Indiana University Press.

———, ed. 1981. *The Evil Eye: A Folklore Casebook*. New York: Garland.

Efimenko, P. S. 1874. *Sbornik malorossiiskikh zaklinanii* (Collection of Little Russian [Ukrainian] incantations). Moscow: Obshchestvo istorii i drevnostei rossiiskikh.

Ehrenreich, Barbara and Deirdre English. 1973. *Witches, Midwives, and Nurses: A History of Women Healers*. [Old Westbury, N. Y.:] Feminist Press.

Foster, George M. 1976. "Disease Etiologies in Non-Western Medical Systems." *American Anthropologist* 78: 773–82.

——— and Barbara Gallatin Anderson. 1978. *Medical Anthropology*. New York: John Wiley and Sons.

Frank, Jerome D. 1959. "The Dynamics of a Psychotherapeutic Relationship: Determinants and Effects of the Therapist's Influence." *Psychiatry* 22: 17–39.

———. 1973. *Persuasion and Healing: A Comparative Study of Psychotherapy*. Baltimore: The Johns Hopkins University Press.

Franko, Ivan, comp. 1898. "Hutsul's'ki prymivky" (Hutsul incantations). *Etnohrafichnyi zbirnyk* 5: 41–72.

Galay, Ted. 1981. *After Baba's Funeral* and *Sweet and Sour Pickles: Two Plays by Ted Galay*. Toronto: Playwrights Canada.

Gulutsan, Lena Hryhor. 1978. *Deedo's Children: A Story of John Hryhor of Nipawin, Saskatchewan*. Edmonton: the author.

Hanchuk, Rena. 1984a. "A Comparative Study of Folk Medicine in the Ukrainian-Canadian Context: The Wax Ceremony." Student essay for UKR 660. University of Alberta.

———. 1984b. "Fortune-Telling in the Canadian-Ukrainian Context: The Wax Ceremony, a Documentation and Analysis." Student essay for UKR 532. University of Alberta.

Hand, Wayland D. 1980. *Magical Medicine: The Folkloric Component of Medicine in the Folk Belief, Custom, and Ritual of the Peoples of Europe and Asia. Selected Essays*. Berkeley: University of California Press.

Honko, Lauri. 1964. "On the Effectivity of Folk Medicine." In *Papers on Folk Medicine Given at an Inter-Nordic Symposium at Nordiska museet, Stockholm, 8–10 May 1961*, edited by Carl-Herman Tillhagen, 290–300. Stockholm: The Nordic Museum.

Ilarion, Metropolitan [Ohiienko, Ivan]. 1965. *Dokhrystyians'ki viruvannia ukraïns'koho narodu* (Pre-Christian beliefs of the Ukrainian people). Winnipeg: Volyn'.

Jones, Michael. 1972. *Why Faith Healing?* Ottawa: National Museum of Man.

K., V. 1902. "'Liky' moego sela" ("Cures" of my village). *Kievskaia starina* 78, bk. 3, no. 9: 319–42.

Kemp, P. 1935. *Studies in the Technique and Tradition of the Southern Slavs*. London: Faber and Faber.

Kertselli, N. G. 1874. "Zametki o narodnoi meditsine v Malorossii" (Observations on folk medicine in Little Russia [Ukraine]). *Izvestiia Obshchestva liubitelei estestvoznaniia, antropologii i etnografii pri Moskovskom universitete* 12. *Trudy etnograficheskogo otdela*, bk. 3: 61–2.

Klymasz, Andrea. 1989. "Ukrainian Folk Medicine in Canada." *Material History Bulletin* (Ottawa) 29 (1989): 99–101.

———. 1991. "Folk Medicine: A Ukrainian Canadian Experience." M.A. thesis, University of Manitoba.

Klymasz, Robert B. 1980. *Ukrainian Folklore in Canada: An Immigrant Complex in Transition*. Ph.D. diss., Indiana University, 1971. New York: Arno Press.

———. 1992. *Sviéto: Celebrating Ukrainian-Canadian Ritual in East Central Alberta through the Generations*. Occasional Paper 21. Edmonton: Historic Sites and Archives Service.

Kolberg, Oskar. [1889] 1963. *Pokucie: Obraz etnograficzny* (Pokuttia: An ethnographic sketch). Vol. 3. Cracow: Uniwersytet Jagielloński. Reprinted as his *Dzieła wszystkie*, vol. 32. Warsaw: Ludowa Spółdzielnia Wydawnicza.

Kolessa, Filiaret. [1938] 1983. *Usna narodna slovesnist'* (Oral folk literature). Edmonton: Canadian Institute of Ukrainian Studies.

Kostash, Myrna. 1980. *All of Baba's Children*. Edmonton: Hurtig Publishers.

Kovalenko, G., and I. Manzhura. 1891. "O narodnoi meditsine v Pereiaslavskom uezde Poltavskoi gubernii" (On folk medicine in Pereiaslav county of Poltava province). *Etnograficheskoe obozrenie* 9: 141–9.

Kylymnyk, Stepan. 1963. *Ukraïns'kyi rik u narodnikh zvychaiakh v istorychnomu osvitlenni* (The Ukrainian year in folk customs in historical light). Vol. 5. *Osinnii tsykl'* (The autumn cycle). Winnipeg: Ukraïns'kyi natsional'nyi vydavnychyi komitet.

Lepkii, Daniyl. 1884. "Pro narodni zabobony" (On folk superstitions). *Zoria*, no. 13: 105–7; no. 15–16: 123–4.

Lysenko, Vera. 1954. *Yellow Boots*. Toronto: Ryerson Press.

Madsen, William, and Claudia Madsen. 1972. *A Guide to Mexican Witchcraft*. Mexico: Minutiae Mexicana.

Malinowski, Bronislaw. 1954. "Magic, Science, and Religion," and Other Essays. New York: Doubleday Anchor Books.

Maloney, Clarence, ed. 1976. *The Evil Eye*. New York: Columbia University Press.

Martynowych, Orest. 1991. *Ukrainians in Canada: The Formative Period, 1891–1927*. Edmonton: Canadian Institute of Ukrainian Studies Press.

Mealing, F. M. 1972. "Our People's Way: A Study of Doukhobor Hymnody and Folklife." Ph.D. diss., University of Pennsylvania.

Miloradovich, V. 1900. "Narodnaia meditsina v Lubenskom uezde, Poltavskoi gubernii" (Folk medicine in Lubni county, Poltava province). *Kievskaia starina* 68, bk. 1: 46–61; bk. 2: 192–206; bk.3: 373–95; 69, bk. 2: 160–73; bk. 3: 310–32; 70, bk. 1–2: 51–65.

Min'ko, L. I. 1969. *Narodnaia meditsina Belorussii* (Folk medicine of Belarus). Minsk: Nauka i tekhnika.

Miroliubov, Iurii. 1982. *Russkii iazycheskii fol'klor: Ocherki byta i nravov* (Russian pagan folklore: Sketches of folkways and customs). Munich: Otto Sagner.

Moore, Omar. 1957. "Divination: A New Perspective." *American Anthropologist* 59: 69–74.

Moszyński, Kazimierz. [1934] 1967. "Medycyna" (Medicine). In his *Kultura ludowa słowian* (Slavic folk culture). Vol. 2, part 1: 175–232. Warsaw: Książka i Wiedza.

Mushynka, Mykola, comp. 1967. *Z hlybyny vikiv* (From the depths of the ages). Bratislava: Slovenské pedagogické nakladatel'stvo.

Myerhoff, Barbara. 1976. "Shamanic Equilibrium: Balance and Mediation in Known and Unknown Worlds." In *American Folk Medicine: A Symposium*, edited by Wayland D. Hand, 99–108. Berkeley: University of California Press.

Nechui-Viter, A. (Hanna Barvinok). 1861. "Ne bulo zmalku—ne bude i dostanku" (If you didn't have it in youth—you won't get it later). *Osnova* (St. Petersburg), no. 6: 17–46.

Nedzel's'kyi, Ievhen, comp. 1955. *Z ust narodu* (From the mouths of the people) Prešov: Kul'turna spilka ukraïns'kykh trudiashchykh.

"Novinki: Sueverie" (News: Superstition). 1893. *Galichanin* (Lviv), no. 20: 3.

Onats'kyi, Ievhen. 1957. "Visk" (Wax). In his *Ukraïns'ka mala entsyklopediia* (The little Ukrainian encyclopedia), 179. Buenos Aires: Ukraïns'ka Avtokefal'na Pravoslavna Tserkva v Argentini.

———. 1964. "Svichka" (Candle). In his *Ukraïns'ka mala entsyklopediia* (The little Ukrainian encyclopedia), 1697–1700. Buenos Aires: Ukrains'ka Avtokefal'na Pravoslavna Tserkva v Argentini.

Petroff, Louis. 1957. "Magical Beliefs and Practises in Old Bulgaria." *Mid-West Folklore* 7: 214–20.

Petrov, V. 1963. "Elements of Pre-Christian Religion and the People's

View of Life." In *Ukraine: A Concise Encyclopaedia*, vol. 1, edited by Volodymyr Kubijovyč, 341–6. Toronto: University of Toronto Press.

Podolinskii, S. 1879. "Zdorov'e krestian na Ukraine" (The health of peasants in Ukraine). *Delo*, no. 5: 146–89.

Pondoev, Gavriil S. 1959. *Notes of a Soviet Doctor*. Translated by Basil Haigh. London: Chapman Hall.

Porits'kyi, A. Ia. and A. M. Prykhod'ko. 1965. "Vyvchaimo narodnu medytsynu" (Let's study folk medicine). *Narodna tvorchist' ta etnohrafiia*, no. 4: 69–72.

Ralston, William R. S. [1872] 1970. *The Songs of the Russian People*. New York: Haskell House.

Red'ko, A. 1899. "Nechistaia sila v sud'bakh zhenshchiny-materi (The evil force in the destiny of the woman-mother). *Etnograficheskoe obozrenie* 40, no. 1–2: 54–132.

Russell, Louise. 1981. "Conversation with a Curandera." In *Folklore Women's Communication* 21: 11–12.

Samuels, Victor [Victor J. Banis]. 1970. *Charms, Spells, and Curses*. Los Angeles: Sherbourne Press.

Shukhevych, Volodymyr. 1908. *Hutsul'shchyna* (The Hutsul region). Vol. 5. Lviv: Zahal'na drukarnia.

Shumovs'kyi, P. 1955. "Kul't vody ta ioho znachennia v zhytti liudyny" (The cult of water and its meaning in human life). *Vira i kul'tura*, no. 21: 19–21; no. 25: 14–16.

Sokolov, Iurii M. 1950. *Russian Folklore*. Translated by Catherine Ruth Smith. New York: Macmillan.

Stein, Howard, F. 1976. "Envy and the Evil Eye: An Essay on the Psychological Ontogeny of Belief and Ritual." In *The Evil Eye*, edited by Clarence Maloney, 193–222. New York: Columbia Press.

Steinfirst, Susan. 1992. *Folklore and Folklife: A Guide to English Language Reference Sources*. 2 vols. New York: Garland.

Subtelny, Orest. 1988. *Ukraine: A History*. Toronto: University of Toronto Press.

Tarasoff, Koozma. 1977. *Traditional Doukhobor Folkways: An Ethnographic and Biographic Record of Prescribed Behavior*. Ottawa: National Museum of Canada.

Tesla, I. et al. "XIII. Ukrainians Abroad: 3. In Canada." 1971. In *Ukraine: A Concise Encyclopaedia,* vol. 2, edited by Volodymyr Kubijovyč, 1151–93. Toronto: University of Toronto Press.

Thompson, C. J. S. 1946. *Magic and Healing.* London: Rider and Company.

Tillich, Paul. 1946. "The Relation of Religion and Health: Historical Considerations and Theoretical Questions." *Review of Religion* 10: 348–84.

Tokarev, S. A. 1957. *Religioznye verovaniia vostochnoslavianskikh narodov XIX–nachala XX v.* (Religious beliefs of the East Slavic peoples in the nineteenth–beginning of the twentieth centuries). Moscow: Izdatel'stvo Akademii nauk SSSR.

Toelken, Barre. 1979. *The Dynamics of Folklore.* Boston: Houghton Mifflin.

Vovk, Khvedir. [1928] 1976. *Studii z ukraïns'koï etnohrafiï ta antropolohiï* (Studies in Ukrainian ethnography and anthropology). New York: Howerla.

Voropai, Oleksa. 1958–66. *Zvychaï nashoho narodu* (Customs of our people). 2 vols. Munich: Ukraïns'ke vydavnytstvo.

Weatherhead, Leslie D. 1952. *Psychology, Religion, and Healing.* New York: Abingdon Press.

Yoder, Don. 1972. "Folk Medicine." In *Folklore and Folklife: An Introduction,* edited by Richard M. Dorson, 191–215. Chicago: University of Chicago Press.

Index

n=note; t=table